TOP **10**
LISBON

T0182261

CONTENTS

LISBON

INTRODUCING

The Arco da Rua Augusta

WELCOME TO
LISBON

Hours are spent in Lisbon getting lost in historic neighbourhoods, listening to soulful *fado* music and watching the sunset from the city's hilltops. Don't want to miss a thing? With Top 10 Lisbon, you'll enjoy the very best the city has to offer.

With nearly 3,000 hours of sunshine a year, the best way to explore Lisbon is, quite simply, by being outside. The city bursts with green parks, where you can enjoy a morning *bica* (espresso) at a traditional kiosk and take in the fresh air, while the hilltops are studded with *miradouros*, providing spectacular views of architectural beauties like the Sé de Lisboa and Castelo de São Jorge. Wander along the maze of steep, narrow streets and take photographs of *azulejos*-adorned façades, or travel by tram to soak up picturesque

Traditional tram in Lisbon

districts like historic Alfama with its medieval street plan still largely intact. However you choose to spend your day, it will likely be punctuated with stop-offs at *pastelarias* (pastry shops) for an iconic *pastel de nata* or two. Come evening, the bars in the lively districts of Bairro Alto and Cais do Sodrè sprawl out their streetside tables, ready for evenings ahead of bar-hopping fun.

While the city centre has a lot going for it, it's well worth wandering off the beaten track, with plenty of options within easy reach. Travel west to Belém and you'll find imposing monuments like Mosteiro dos Jerónimos and, along the riverside, the Torre de Belém; both were built from the profits of Portugal's maritime expeditions in the 16th century. Hop on a train to the village of Sintra – much of it is a designated UNESCO World Heritage Site – to explore fairytale-like palaces nestled amid a forest or hit the coast to enjoy a barefoot stroll along the sprawling golden beaches that hug the seaside town of Cascais, located to the southwest of Lisbon's city centre.

So, where to start? With Top 10 Lisbon, of course. This pocket-sized guide gets to the heart of the city with simple lists of 10, expert local knowledge and comprehensive maps, helping you turn an ordinary trip into an extraordinary one.

THE STORY OF
LISBON

Lisbon's strategic point by the water helped it become a thriving port for centuries. Portugal's capital city has experienced sieges, grown into a controversial trading hub, and crumbled over an economic crisis, only to be reborn again. Here's the story of how it came to be.

Lisbon Rises

The first settlements in Lisbon date back to the Palaeolithic Age, but it was in the Iron Age that the city began developing its port. Its privileged location, between the Tagus River and the Atlantic, made it a coveted base for civilizations such as the Phoenicians, the Greeks and the Romans. In 138 BCE, the Romans set foot in Lisbon (known at the time as Olissipo), and established it as the administrative capital of Lusitania, an ancient Roman province covering part of Spain and Portugal.

After establishing themselves as the city's official rulers, they built a theatre above one of its hills (remnants of which can still be seen today) and ruled for seven centuries. Then, in 711 CE, the Moors took over, renaming the city al-Uxbuna. Their reign ended in 1147 when Afonso Henriques, the king of the newly formed kingdom of Portugal, claimed the city, surrounding it with his crusaders and thus beginning Christian rule. Soon, Lisbon became Portugal's capital, leading to a growth in population and expansion of territory.

Breaking Borders

Not content with the size of their empire, Portugal's kings sought to explore beyond the Atlantic, using Lisbon as their departure point. In 1415, the Portuguese began the first of many maritime expeditions by invading Ceuta on the north coast of

Oil painting of *The Siege of Lisbon*, by Joaquim Rodrigues Braga

Illustration of the Mosteiro dos Jerónimos in Belém

Africa. Other trips followed suit, expanding Portugal's empire to far-off lands, such as Brazil and India, and establishing trading routes that made the country richer than ever. The sudden wealth brought by the so-called "Age of Discovery" is what led to the construction of extravagant monuments like the Mosteiro dos Jerónimos in Belém. But this overseas expansion came at a price: lands were seized from native people, many of whom became slaves to the empire.

On Shaky Ground

Portugal and its capital seemed unstoppable – until the day King Sebastião went missing in a battle in Alcácer Quibir, around 1578. Left without a ruler, the country lost its independence to Spain, only to regain it in 1640. With the help of Brazilian gold, Lisbon was soon back on its feet, erecting palaces and establishing its first water supply system fed by the Aqueduto das Águas Livres. Just as things were finally looking up, on 1 November 1755 a massive earthquake hit the city, quickly followed by a tsunami and a fire. Lisbon's downtown was completely ravaged, and many of its prominent buildings collapsed, like the Igreja do Carmo, whose roofless church still serves as a reminder of the event. Marquês de Pombal, then Portugal's chief minister, was responsible for piecing the city back together and mapping out the Lisbon you see today.

Moments in History

1200 BCE
Phoenicians found a trading post they call Allis Ubbo ("safe port").

711 CE
Moorish invaders from North Africa colonize the city.

1147
Christian Crusaders seize control of the Castelo de São Jorge from the Moors in the "Conquest of Lisbon".

1415
The Portuguese begin their first maritime expeditions, setting sail from Lisbon to Ceuta in Northern Africa.

1755
A violent earthquake, followed by a tsunami and a fire, bring the capital to its knees, destroying much of the downtown.

1807–11
Napoleon's army invades, and the monarchy flees to Brazil.

1910
Manuel II, the last king of Portugal, is exiled to Britain as Portugal is declared a republic.

1974
Nearly half a century after the start of Portugal's dictatorship rule, the government finally collapses after the Carnation Revolution.

1986
Portuguese politics stabilizes and on 1 January Portugal becomes a member of the European Union.

2023
Around 30,000 million people visit Portugal this year; the capital is among the country's top picks, a clear sign of its booming tourism industry.

The City Rebels

It was Marquês de Pombal who sparked for the extinction of the country's religious orders; he expelled the Jesuits from Portugal, marking the end of what was considered to be the excessive economic and social power of the clergy. This marked a move towards the Enlightenment – essentially a move away from religion – which went on to lay the foundations for the city's industrialization. By the 19th century, Lisbon had transformed, with an active railway and factories producing textiles, tobacco and conserved goods. Still, there was an underlying instability in the city, marked first by the conflicts between absolutists (those who wanted the king to have absolute power) and liberals (those with different ideas on how the country should be ruled and its constitution).

When Portuguese King Carlos and his heir Prince Luís Filipe were assassinated in 1908 outside Terreiro do Paço, it signalled the end of an era. Two years later, Lisbon was officially part of a republic – but not for long. Portugal fell into the hands of the ruthless

political agitator António Salazar, and entered an oppressive dictatorship that would last nearly 50 years.

While the rest of Europe was at war in the early 20th century, Lisbon lived in a seemingly introspective position, erecting statues of figures of the past, commissioning tapestries of its monuments and throwing parades in honour of Santo António, the city's patron saint. But at the same time, secret meetings were being held underground, by artists, writers and the general public who conspired against Salazar's totalitarian regime for freedom of speech. On 25 April 1974, as the song "Grândola, Vila Morena" played on the radio, the people hit the streets in a coup known as the Carnation Revolution, which effectively marked the end of Salazar and his dictatorship.

Lisbon Today

Unchained at last, it was clear that Lisbon hadn't quite progressed as much as its neighbouring European capitals, and suffered major housing issues as a result.

Exterior of the Museum of Art, Architecture and Technology (MAAT)

Initially, Lisbon struggled to keep up, especially as much of its population emigrated between the 1970s and 80s in search of better job opportunities – a phenomenon still felt today. However, when Portugal joined the European Union in 1986, it gained access to funds that helped rejuvenate its capital and housing conditions, so much so that Lisbon hosted its own World Exhibition in 1998, kick-starting tourist interest.

The 2008 financial crisis and later the COVID-19 pandemic destabilized the country's economy, but largely thanks to tourism and a growing investment in the tech and start-up scene, the city has become an exciting hub for remote workers and sun-seeking travellers. Today the Portuguese capital is one of the most popular city-break destinations in Europe.

Photograph of the Carnation Revolution on 25 April 1974

TOP 10
EXPERIENCES

Planning the perfect trip to Lisbon? Whether you're visiting for the first time or making a return trip, there are some things you simply shouldn't miss out on. To make the most of your time – and to enjoy the very best this charmingly laid-back city has to offer – be sure to add these experiences to your list.

1 Magical miradouros
Sprawling over a sea of hills, Lisbon offers countless viewpoints, known as *miradouros*. These popular hangouts see Lisboetas toast to the city's magical sunsets; you'll find some of the best at Miradouro da Senhora do Monte (p49), Miradouro de Santa Catarina (p48) and Miradouro de Santa Luzia (p48).

2 Perfect pastéis de nata
Tuck into Lisbon's most iconic treat, the *pastel de nata*, a delicious custard tart featured in every *pastelaria* (pastry shop) in town. For the original, and some say still the best, make a beeline to Antiga Confeitaria de Belém (*pasteisdebelem.pt*), where you can satiate your sweet tooth.

3 Gaze at azulejos
Colourful *azulejos* (tiles) adorn Lisbon's numerous façades, churches and underground stations, transforming the city into an open-air gallery. To learn more about this traditional craft (and get a glimpse of pre-earthquake Lisbon), visit the Museu Nacional do Azulejo (p34).

4 Hop on a tram
Winding through the city's narrow streets, the yellow trams are a quintessential Lisbon feature. The famous 28 tram takes visitors through popular neighbourhoods like Chiado (p80) and Alfama (p66), but there's plenty of other routes worth taking to get off the beaten track.

5 Game day

Two of the country's top football teams are based in Lisbon: Benfica and Sporting Lisbon (where Cristiano Ronaldo launched his career). The Portuguese worship football, and there's nothing like seeing a game (p96) to feel their enthusiasm.

6 Bar hop in Bairro Alto

Come the weekend, locals flock to Bairro Alto for a night out. This lively district is packed with bars (p86), before the party continues down the street in neighbouring Cais do Sodré, where revellers hit the clubs on Rua Nova do Carvalho (Pink Street; p57).

7 Unwind at a kiosk

Kiosks are dotted all over the city; find one along the river, on a square or hidden inside gardens. Locals love gathering around these Art Nouveau-style huts for their morning *bica* (espresso) or an after-work *imperial* (small beer).

8 Listen to fado

Fado is a traditional Portuguese music genre that originated in Alfama (p66). The lyrics often approach the feeling of saudade, a sense of nostalgia. Catching a live performance at a *fado* house (p57) is always a memorable event.

9 Take a walk through city history

Part of the experience of visiting Lisbon is winding through its maze of streets. Join a street art or history walking tour, like the African Lisbon Tour (p73) or the Lisbon Street Art Tours (lisbonstreetarttours.com).

10 Retreat to the beach

Take a train along Lisbon's coast to Cascais (p101) for a refreshing swim in the Atlantic (be warned, the water is deceptively cold). Or, take the ferry and head south across the river to the surf-friendly beaches of Costa da Caparica.

ITINERARIES

Seeing the *azulejos*-adorned façades, travelling the tram-lined streets, visiting the Sé de Lisboa: there's a lot to see and do in Lisbon. With places to eat, drink or simply take in the view, these itineraries offer ways to spend 2 days and 4 days in the city.

2 DAYS

Day 1

Morning
Start your day by tackling the hilly Chiado district. First, enjoy a *bica* (espresso) at A Brasileira (*p85*), an Art Nouveau café where Portuguese poet Fernando Pessoa was a regular. Then walk east, up Calçada do Sacramento towards the Igreja do Carmo (*p83*), whose roofless patio serves as a reminder of the 1755 earthquake that ravaged the city. Around the corner is the striking Elevador de Santa Justa (*p75*), a Neo-Gothic lift built in 1902 that connects the lower streets with Largo do Carmo. Take the nearby steps that head downhill and stroll along Rua Augusta, stopping for lunch at Prado (*p79*).

EAT
A visit to Belém wouldn't be complete without sampling the original *pastel de nata*, Lisbon's beloved custard tart. The Pastéis de Belém (*p92*) has been baking fresh batches of these since 1837.

Afternoon
Continue east to Alfama, the city's oldest neighbourhood, to reach the Sé de Lisboa (*p26*). Step inside to gaze at the cathedral's Romanesque nave and its rose window before walking to Castelo de São Jorge (*p22*), which sits on the crown of the hill. Make the most of its Moorish legacy and architecture, and gaze over the maze of traditional cafés, houses and *fado* restaurants below. Ready for dinner? Just around the corner you'll find Arco do Castelo (*p71*), where you can tuck into tasty Goan specialities.

Day 2

Morning
Spend your morning touring the monument-filled neighbourhood of Belém. Start at the Mosteiro dos Jerónimos (*p24*), a striking 16th-century monastery funded by a spice tax introduced when the Portuguese landed in India. The building is a prime example of Manueline architecture, drawing much of its inspiration from nautical elements linked to Portugal's maritime explorations. Along the riverfront, the

Inside A Brasileria, one of Lisbon's most famous cafés

Torre de Belém (p32) was built around the same time, erected to guard the monastery and Lisbon's port against pirate raids. Rest your legs with a ride on the tram until you reach Canalha (Rua da Junqueira 207), a modern seafood restaurant run by acclaimed chef João Rodrigues.

Afternoon
Across from Canalha lies MAAT (p44), a modern art museum; take in its cutting-edge temporary exhibitions before climbing up to the undulating rooftop for panoramic river views. Then, hop on a tram to the Museu Nacional de Arte Antiga (p28) to admire Portugal's national art collection. Walk west from the museum to the LX Factory (lxfactory. com), a former textile factory turned creative hub. End the evening here, browsing through pretty bookstores like Ler Devagar (lerdevagar.com), before enjoying a well-earned dinner at one of the surrounding restaurants.

Browsing the selection of books at one of the stores at the LX Factory

> 📷 **VIEW**
> Stand at the edge of Largo da Sé in Alfama to witness the iconic 28 tram gliding through with the cathedral in the background. Its brilliant-yellow exterior makes for a great photo, too.

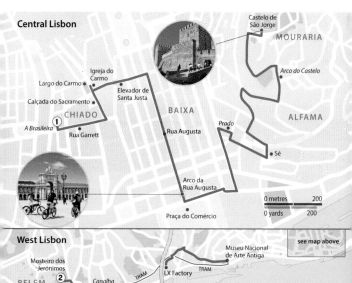

Central Lisbon

Castelo de São Jorge

MOURARIA

Arco do Castelo

Igreja do Carmo

Largo do Carmo

Elevador de Santa Justa

Calçada do Sacramento

CHIADO

A Brasileira ①

Rua Garrett

BAIXA

Prado

Rua Augusta

ALFAMA

Sé

Arco da Rua Augusta

0 metres 200
0 yards 200

Praça do Comércio

West Lisbon

see map above

Museu Nacional de Arte Antiga

Mosteiro dos Jerónimos

BELÉM ②

Canalha

TRAM

TRAM

LX Factory

TRAM

TRAM

MAAT

Torre de Belém

0 km 1
0 miles 1

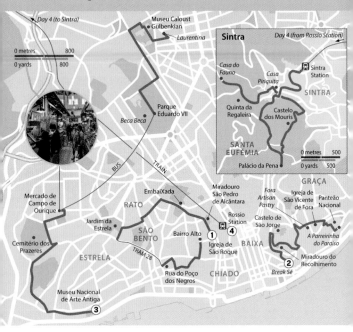

4 DAYS

Day 1

Begin the day at Igreja de São Roque (p81), which houses one of Europe's most expensive chapels. It was built in the 16th century using the most precious material available at the time. Once you've been suitably wowed, continue uphill towards the Miradouro São Pedro de Alcântara for a postcard view of Lisbon's castle. It's a short walk from here to Embaixada (p84), a Neo-Moorish palace now filled with shops run by Portuguese makers; while away the

Bustling Bairro Alto known for its mix of tapas restaurants and bars

rest of the morning here. Take the 28 tram from nearby Jardim da Estrela (p61) to trendy Rua do Poço dos Negros for lunch and then hit Bairro Alto for top tapas and bars in the evening.

Day 2

After a leisurely brunch at Break Sé (Rua da Saudade 2A), kick-start your day at

---

🚌 **TRANSPORT**
When buying public transport tickets, choose the Zapping option. This is a rechargeable ticket that provides rides on buses, trams and train rides, including the train journey to Sintra.

☕ **DRINK**
On your way back from Sintra, head to A Ginjinha (p78), near the Rossio train station, to sample Lisbon's traditional sour cherry liqueur.

the Castelo de São Jorge (p22). Its hilltop location is a great place to get your bearings, and just around the corner lies the Miradouro do Recolhimento; from its hexagonal-shaped seat, you can take in more sweeping views. It's a relatively short walk from the viewpoint to the Igreja de São Vicente de Fora (p46), a 16th-century church that contains the stone sarcophagi of almost every Portuguese king and queen. Most visit to check out the impressive collection of azulejos, too. After a brief bica at Fora Artisan Pastry (Calçada de São Vicente 95), a short walk away takes you to the Panteão Nacional (p68). This landmark building is the final resting place of the late fado singer Amália Rodrigues. End with dinner at A Parreirinha do Paraíso (Rua do Paraíso 40C).

Day 3

Begin by exploring the European art collection at Museu Nacional de Arte Antiga (p28), which contains a whopping 40,000 works of art. Head north towards Cemitério dos Prazeres, a local cemetery offering amazing views of the Ponte 25 de Abril, which doesn't look too dissimilar from San Francisco's Golden Gate Bridge. For lunch, drop into the nearby Mercado de Campo de Ourique, a food market serving everything from ramen to BBQ chicken. Next, take a brief bus ride north to Parque Eduardo VII (p95), where you'll find the Beca Beca kiosk, ideal for a quick respite. Spend the rest of the afternoon exploring the staggering works on display at the Museu Calouste Gulbenkian (p38), which holds the private art collection of Armenian oil magnate Calouste Gulbenkian. For dinner, enjoy bacalhau just across the street at Laurentina (p99).

Day 4

Journey from Rossio train station to the village of Sintra (p40). Once there, take the bus (or if you're feeling adventurous, hike – make sure you wear sturdy walking shoes) up to Palácio da Pena. With its bright-coloured walls emerging amid the hills, this former royal palace looks straight out of a fairytale. From here, it's mostly downhill to the Castelo dos Mouros, whose battlements offer superb views of the surrounding mountains. Have lunch at one of the local restaurants in the town centre, saving room for dessert at Casa Piriquita (p41), which specializes in traditional pastries like travesseiros (pillow-shaped pastries with a sweet almond and egg-yolk filling). Then, venture off to the Quinta da Regaleira, a majestic park filled with grottoes and fountains. A few steps from here is the Casa do Fauno (Caminho dos Frades 1), a medieval-style pub where you can relive bygone days, sipping honey mead or a fresh pint of cider.

The 8th-century Castelo dos Mouros in Sintra

TOP 10 HIGHLIGHTS

Azenhas do Mar, Sintra

EXPLORE THE
HIGHLIGHTS

There are some sights in Lisbon you simply shouldn't miss, and it's these attractions that make the Top 10. Discover what makes each one a must-see on the following pages.

Parque Florestal de Monsanto

AUTOSTRADA DA COSTA DO ESTRIL

BAIRRO DA AJUDA

AVENIDA DE CEUTA

AVENIDA DA PONTE

R.DE CASCAIS

RUA DO CRUZEIRO

RESTELO

AVENIDA DO RESTELO

SANTO AMARO

Jardim Botânico Tropical

2

RUA DA JUNQUEIRA

BELÉM

AVENIDA DA INDIA

AVENIDA DA INDIA

PONTE 25 DE ABRIL

6

0 metres	800
0 yards	800

Greater Lisbon

Agualva-Cacém
Belas
Amadora
Alcabideche

See main map area

0 km 5
0 miles 5

SALDANHA

CAMPOLIDE

Parque Eduardo VII

ESTEFÂNIA

PRAÇA MARQUÊS DE POMBAL

AV. ENGENHEIRO D. PACHECO

AVENIDA DA LIBERDADE

Jardim Botânico

PRAÇA DO PRÍNCIPE REAL

BAIXA

CALÇADA DA ESTRELA

BAIRRO ALTO

RUA DA PRATA

RUA ÁUREA

ESTRELA

CHIADO

PRAÇA DO COMÉRCIO

AVENIDA INFANTE SANTO

Tejo

ALMADA

PRAGAL

❶ Castelo de São Jorge

❷ Mosteiro dos Jeronimos

❸ Sé de Lisboa

❹ Museu Nacional de Arte Antiga

❺ Parque das Nações

❻ Torre de Belém

❼ Museu Nacional do Azulejo

❽ Palácio Nacional de Queluz

❾ Museu Calouste Gulbenkian

❿ Sintra

CASTELO DE SÃO JORGE

📍 G4 🏛 Porta de São Jorge, Rua de Santa Cruz do Castelo ⏰ Main castle complex: 9am–9pm daily (Nov–Feb: to 6pm) 🌐 castelodesaojorge.pt 📱

This hilltop castle is traditionally regarded as the site of Lisbon's founding settlement, although much of the present castle dates from a 1930s restoration. Towering above central Lisbon, it's one of the city's most recognizable landmarks.

1 Porta de São Jorge

⏰ 9am–9pm daily (Nov–Feb: to 6pm) 📱

This grand gate leads onto the final steep climb up to the castle grounds. In a wall niche to the left is a figure of St George.

2 Torre da Igreja

⏰ 10am–1pm & 2–6pm daily 📱

This 18th-century church tower on Largo de Santa Cruz do Castelo was closed and largely forgotten until 2018. A separate ticket gives you access to the top for incredible city views.

3 Torre de Ulisses

⏰ 10am–5pm daily (Oct–Mar: to 2pm)

In one of the inner battlement towers, a camera obscura attached to a periscope projects images of the city. The castle has a history of distant gazing: Lisbon's first observatory was set up here in around 1788.

4 Castle Museum

⏰ 9am–8pm daily (Nov–Feb: to 6pm) 📱

On the site of the Alcáçovas palace, this museum contains a collection of artifacts excavated from the hilltop, such as Iron Age pots and 15th-century tiles.

☕ **DRINK**
The outdoor bar at Chapitô café (p70) is the perfect place to enjoy a drink and soak up fantastic views of the city.

Excavated artifacts at the castle museum

50 metres (55 yards)

FLORES DE S. CRUZ

S. CRUZ DO CASTELO

RECOLHIMENTO

Castelo de São Jorge Site Map

Castelo de São Jorge looming above the city

5 Torre de São Lourenço

Connected to the castle by a long series of steps, this tower once formed part of the outer fortifications. Today, it offers another angle from which to view the castle.

6 Santa Cruz Neighbourhood

The tiny neighbourhood of Santa Cruz do Castelo, within the old citadel, is one of the most picturesque parts of Lisbon. It is home to cafés, guesthouses and a viewpoint overlooking Alfama.

7 Inner Battlements

The reconstruction of the inner castle is one of the great achievements of the 1938 restoration. With ten towers and a dividing inner wall, the restored castle closely matches the layout and size of the original.

8 Archaeological Site

This site features traces of the most significant periods in Lisbon's history, including settlements from the Iron Age.

9 Statue of Afonso Henriques

This bronze statue of Portugal's first king was added to the esplanade in 1947. It is a replica of an 1887 work by Soares dos Reis (the original is in Guimarães).

10 Esplanade

The esplanade on top of the outer fortifications is one of the main rewards of a climb up to the castle. Dotted with archaeological remains and shaded by pines, it follows the castle's western perimeter, offering views of the river and lower city.

Bronze statue of Afonso Henriques

PORTA DE MARTIM MONIZ

According to legend, the knight Martim Moniz prevented this gate from closing with his own body, sacrificing his life to allow Afonso Henriques and his troops to storm the castle. The gate where his unverified deed took place bears his name, as does a square below the castle.

MOSTEIRO DOS JERÓNIMOS

📍 B6 🏛 Praça do Império, Belém 🕐 9:30am–6pm Tue–Sun 🚫 1 Jan, Easter Sun, 1 May, 13 Jun & 25 Dec 🌐 mosteirojeronimos.gov.pt 🔗

Few of Lisbon's monuments are overly grand, and while this historic monastery is imposing, it's easy to explore. Complete with twisted columns and maritime motifs, the Mosteiro dos Jerónimos expresses a uniquely national style, symbolizing Portugal's colonial conquests and imperial ambitions.

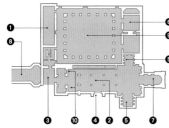

Mosteiro dos Jerónimos Floorplan

1 Refectory
The long, narrow refectory features fabulous vaulting and rope-like Manueline mouldings. The panel on the north wall depicts the biblical story of the feeding of the 5,000.

2 Nave
Many visitors find the well-lit nave the most striking feature of Jerónimos, with its soaring carved pillars supporting a beautiful fan-vaulted ceiling.

3 West Portal
The surrounds of this portal (now the main entrance) were sculpted by Nicolau Chanterène, and show the Manueline love of fantastical Renaissance decoration.

4 South Portal
Restraint might not be the word for this towering sculpture

Ribbed ceiling and *azulejo* tile walls in the refectory

of an entrance, but look closely and you'll see that none of its parts are overpoweringly large. The figures include Henry the Navigator.

5 Tombs of Dom Sebastião and Cardinal D. Henrique
As you pass under the stellar vault of the crossing, look to each side to see the grand tombs of Cardinal D. Henrique and the young king Dom Sebastião.

6 Chapterhouse
Completed only in the 19th century, the attractive chapterhouse was never used as such. It houses the tomb of Alexandre Herculano, a celebrated 19th-century historian who also served as the first mayor of Belém.

7 Main Chapel
The current main chapel, dating from 1572, has a grid-like Mannerist layout. Look out for the tombs of

Manueline cloisters adorned with richly carved arches

Dom Manuel I and his wife Dona Maria (on the left) and Dom João III and his wife Dona Catarina (on the right).

8 Extension

Major restoration works in the 19th century added the long, Neo-Manueline west wing, which now houses the Museu de Arqueologia (closed for renovation until 2025) and part of the Museu de Marinha. A distinctive domed bell tower was built to replace the previous pointed roof.

9 Cloister

The unique two-storey cloister is a lesson in Manueline tracery and lavish ornament. Fernando Pessoa (p89), the renowned poet, is buried in the cloister.

10 Tombs of Vasco da Gama and Luís de Camões

In the Lower Choir (facing the aisles under the gallery) are the tombs of Vasco da Gama and Luís de Camões, transferred here in 1898.

STONE SURPRISES

Spend some time studying the carvings on the pillars in the nave and you will come across plants and animals, along with exquisite human faces, and a few mythical figures. What better way to remind posterity that all this beauty was hewn by human hands, belonging to individuals who occasionally let their imaginations roam free while carving.

The 19th-century tomb of navigator Vasco da Gama

SÉ DE LISBOA

📍 G4 🏠 Largo da Sé 🕐 Church: 9:30am–7pm Mon–Sat (Nov–May: 10am–6pm) 🌐 sedelisboa.pt ♿

Lisbon's cathedral was built shortly after Afonso Henriques had taken the city from the Moors in 1147. Today's crenellated Romanesque building is a much-restored reconstruction, rebuilt in various architectural styles following earthquake damage.

Looking down the cathedral's soaring nave

1 Romanesque Nave

Little remains of the original cathedral beyond the renovated nave. It leads to a chancel enclosed by an ambulatory, a 14th-century addition.

2 Treasury

The first-floor Treasury is a museum of religious art, with some important holdings. It lost its greatest treasure, the relics of St Vincent (p46), in the 1755 earthquake.

3 St Anthony's Font

It is believed that Fernando Martins Bulhões (later St Anthony) was baptized in this font, which now features a tile panel of the saint preaching to the fish. He is also said to have attended the cathedral school.

4 Cloister

The Gothic cloister, reached through one of the chapels, was an early addition to the cathedral. Some of its decoration anticipates the Manueline style. Head for the lighter cloister, and try to go in the afternoon, when the low light enters the rose window. Ongoing excavations in the cloister have unearthed various Roman remains.

5 Capela de Bartolomeu Joanes

This Gothic chapel, sponsored by a Lisbon merchant in 1324, has the founder's tomb and a 15th-century Renaissance retable, painted by Cristóvão de Figueiredo, Garcia Fernandes and Diogo de Contreiras.

> ☕ **DRINK**
> A great place for a relaxed drink in the neighbourhood is the medieval-style Crafty Corner (p70), which offers a fine selection of local craft beers.

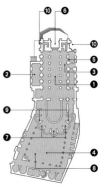

Sé de Lisboa Floorplan

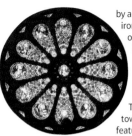

Rose window with Christ as the central figure

6 Rose Window

Reconstructed using parts of the original, the rose window softens the façade's rather severe aspect. It depicts Jesus surrounded by the 12 apostles.

7 Gothic Ambulatory Chapels

The Chapel of São Cosme and São Damião is one of nine along the ambulatory. Look out for the tombs of nobleman Lopo Fernandes Pacheco and his wife, Maria Villalobos.

8 Archaeological Finds

Remains left by Moors, Visigoths, Romans and Phoenicians have been found in the excavation of the cloister.

9 13th-century Iron Railing

One of the ambulatory chapels is closed off by a 13th-century iron railing, the only one of its kind to survive in Portugal.

10 Bell Towers

These stocky towers – defining features of the Sé de Lisboa – recall those of Coimbra's earlier cathedral, built by the same master builder, Frei Roberto. A taller third tower collapsed during the 1755 earthquake (p9).

FINDS FROM LISBON'S PAST

Archaeologically, the Sé de Lisboa is a work in progress – just like the castle (p22) and many other parts of central Lisbon. All this digging means that an increasing number of ancient remains are being uncovered. Do make a point of asking – you may be treated to a latest discovery.

A yellow tram passing in front of the bell towers

MUSEU NACIONAL DE ARTE ANTIGA

📍 E5 🏠 Rua das Janelas Verdes ⏰ 10am–6pm Tue–Sun 🚫 1 Jan, Easter Sun, 1 May, 13 Jun, 25 Dec 🌐 museudearteantiga.pt ⤢

Housed in a 17th-century palace overlooking the river and port area, Lisbon's Museu Nacional de Arte Antiga (MNAA) is Portugal's national gallery. Inside is a treasure trove of historically illuminating art, including a selection of European art dating from the 12th to the 19th century.

1 Indo-Portuguese Furniture

The most interesting of the museum's furniture collections is the group of Indo-Portuguese pieces. The *contadores* are many-drawered chests that combine orderliness with decorative abandon.

2 Martyrdom of St Sebastian

Painted by Gregório Lopes around 1536, this work was a part of a group of paintings intended to be placed on the altars of the Rotunda of the Convento de Cristo.

3 Chapel of St Albert

🔧 For restoration until 2025

Decorated with *azulejos* and gilded wood

An ornate Indo-Portuguese *contadore*

> ✂ **EAT**
> An alternative to the museum restaurant is the rooftop bar Catch Me *(Jardim 9 de Abril)*, which offers breathtaking views and live music.

carving, this chapel is a prime example of Portuguese Baroque.

4 The Panels of St Vincent

A key Portuguese painting, this polyptych from around 1470 (probably by Nuno Gonçalves) portrays rich and poor in fascinating detail.

Admiring the *Panels of St Vincent*

Watch a live restoration of the *Panels of St Vincent* via a viewing window on the museum's third floor (until 2025).

5 Portuguese and Chinese Ceramics

The museum's 7,500-piece collection of ceramics illustrates the interplay of international trade influences. From the 16th century, Portuguese faïence displays traces of Ming, while Chinese porcelain includes Portuguese coats of arms and other similar motifs.

6 The Temptation of St Anthony

Hieronymus Bosch's three-panelled feast of fear and fantasy, painted around 1500, depicts spiritual torment. It is one of the museum's great treasures – and one of the world's great paintings.

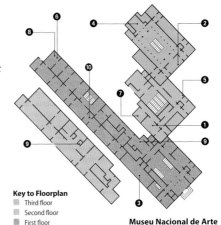

Key to Floorplan
- Third floor
- Second floor
- First floor
- Ground floor

Museu Nacional de Arte Antiga Floorplan

7 Namban Screens

After encountering Portuguese travellers in the 16th century, Japan's artists portrayed them as *namban-jin*, or "southern barbarians". These screens depict the arrival of Portuguese ships in the port of Nagasaki.

8 St Jerome

This unusual portrait of St Jerome transcends the conventions of religious art. Painted in 1521 by Albrecht Dürer – who used a 93-year-old man from Antwerp as his model – it is above all a powerful portrayal of wisdom and old age.

9 Garden, Restaurant and Shop

The museum has a restaurant with lovely views of the garden and the river. There is a gift shop on the first floor.

10 Conversation

Pieter de Hooch was a genre painter whose treatment of light was perhaps more complex than that of his contemporary, Vermeer. This work shows his key qualities as an artist.

TWO CULTURES MEET

Cultural and commercial relations between Portugal and Japan began when three Portuguese travellers were blown off course and drifted onto one of Japan's southern islands in 1543. Fascinated by the Portuguese's colourful clothing and cargo, the Japanese dubbed them *namban-jin*, or "southern barbarians".

Bosch's *The Temptation of St Anthony*

PARQUE DAS NAÇÕES

📍 D1   🏠 Avenida Dom João II

Originally the site of Lisbon's Expo 98 world exposition, the "Park of Nations" is a modern, self-contained riverside district east of the centre. As well as being home to several of Lisbon's top attractions, including Oceanário de Lisboa and Pavilhão do Conhecimento, it also serves as a lively concert and events venue.

2 Restaurants

There are over 40 waterfront restaurants, many with outdoor seating. Popular for weekend lunches, they also form part of the Parque's nightlife scene.

3 Nautical Centre

The Doca dos Olivais nautical centre rents out equipment for various water sports and related activities.

4 Torre Vasco da Gama

At 145 m (476 ft), this is Lisbon's tallest building, albeit removed from the rest of the urban skyline. It is now part of a popular hotel with a Michelin-star restaurant on the top floor.

1 Cable Car

Running most of the length of the Parque, the cable car gives an over-view of the area and views of the river and Vasco da Gama bridge. If the breeze is up, the cars may swing from side to side.

📷 **VIEW**
The brief but fun cable car trip from Torre Vasco da Gama to the marina affords lovely views of the waterfront. It is especially breath-taking at sunset.

5 Oceanário de Lisboa

🕐 10am–8pm daily
🌐 oceanario.pt

One of Europe's largest aquariums, the fasci-nating Oceanário de Lisboa houses hundreds of aquatic species which are organized by habitat and can be viewed on two levels. The central tank has species large and small, but it's the sea otters in a side tank that get the most attention.

Clockwise from top
**Cable cars linking
Torre Vasco da Gama
with the marina;
Centro Vasco da
Gama; Oceanário
de Lisboa**

6 Iberian Lynx by Bordalo II

This giant sculpture (a major photo stop in the area) was created by Bordalo II, one of Portugal's most famous street artists. He is known for his use of rubbish and recycled materials in his pieces.

7 Shops

Most shops are in the Vasco da Gama centre, but there are also electronics and home interiors showrooms elsewhere in the Parque.

8 Pavilhão do Conhecimento

🕙 10am–6pm Tue–Fri, 11am–7pm Sat & Sun 🌐 pavconhecimento.pt 💳

This child-friendly science museum is full of interactive exhibits, simulations, experiments and activities for various age groups.

9 Portugal Pavilion

With its concrete canopy suspended like a sail above the forecourt, the Portugal Pavilion was once meant to house the Council of Ministers.

10 Gardens

Many of the gardens planted for Expo 98 have grown into healthy patches of urban greenery, effectively softening the concrete along the waterfront.

CARD ADVANTAGES

The Lisboa Card ranges in price from €22 (valid for 24 hours) to €46 (72 hours). It provides free transport on the entire network and free entry to 39 places of interest. The card can be bought online at www.visitlisboa.com. A separate card is available for kids.

Panorama of the Parque das Nações on the Tagus

TORRE DE BELÉM

📍 A6 🏠 Avenida Brasília 🕐 10am–5:30pm Tue–Sun (Apr–Sep: to 6:30pm)
🚫 1 Jan, Easter Sun, 1 May, 13 Jun, 24–25 Dec 🌐 torrebelem.com/pt 🔗

Sitting at the edge of the Tagus river, the tower at Belém is a jewel of the Manueline architectural style, combining Moorish, Renaissance and Gothic elements. After admiring the exterior of this elaborate tower, climb its narrow spiral staircase for breathtaking views.

1 Battlements
The merlons of most of the tower's battlements are decorated with the cross of the Order of Christ, carved to look like features on a shield. The smaller merlons at the rear and on top of the tower are crowned with pyramid-shaped spikes.

2 Watchtowers
You can't miss the Moorish-influenced watchtowers. Their domes are seated on Manueline rope-like circles and rise to a pile of small spheres reminiscent of the tops of chess pieces.

3 Exhibitions
The tower's former dungeon, now quite bright, is often used for temporary exhibitions, as well as for a permanent information display for visitors and a gift shop.

> **TOP TIP**
>
> The tower is at its prettiest in the early morning or late afternoon.

4 Virgin and Child Sculpture
A statue of Our Lady of Safe Homecoming stands by the light well that was used to lower cannons into the dungeon. She evokes memories of both Portugal's era of exploration and of those away at sea – and of the concerned longing for absent husbands and sons known in Portugal as *saudade*.

Clockwise from bottom right **Terrace of the Torre de Belém; cannon niches inside the tower; battlements with the cross of the Order of Christ**

Torre de Belém, a fine example of Manueline architecture

5 Governor's Room
Now empty, this room was used by the tower's first governor, Gaspar de Paiva. After it became obsolete, lighthouse keepers and customs officials worked here. The room's acoustics amplify even the slightest whisper.

6 Rhinoceros Detail
Each of the sentry boxes is supported by a carved stone. The rhinoceros on the northwestern box is the most famous, thought to be the first European carving of this animal.

7 Renaissance Loggia
An arcaded loggia overlooks the main deck – comparisons to a ship are unavoidable here. The loggia breaks with the military style of most of the building and adds a theatrical element, while the railing and tracery of the balustrade are pure Manueline. Balconies on each side of the tower echo the loggia's style.

8 Armillary Spheres
The armillary spheres carved above the loggia were instruments for showing the motion of the stars around the earth. They became a symbol of Portugal, and still feature on the national flag.

9 Dungeon
The tower's vaulted bottom level – also used as a dungeon – once housed 17 cannons, which covered the approaches to Lisbon.

10 Manueline Twists
Ropes and knots were the main theme for the Manueline masons here. The tracery of some of the balustrades features the near-organic shapes, that would be developed in later Manueline-style buildings all over the city.

TRANSPORT
A convenient hop-on-hop-off tour bus winds past many of the city's popular landmarks including the Torre de Belém.

HOLY NAMESAKE
Belém means Bethlehem – and the name is taken from a chapel dedicated to St Mary of Bethlehem, built in the mid-15th century near the river's edge, in what was then Restelo. This chapel subsequently gave way to the grand Jerónimos church and monastery; the church is still known as Santa Maria de Belém. The name Restelo, for its part, now applies to the area above and behind Belém, a leafy district of fine residences and embassy buildings.

MUSEU NACIONAL DO AZULEJO

C2   Rua da Madre de Deus 4   10am–1pm & 2–6pm Tue–Sun
1 Jan, Easter Sun, 1 May, 13 Jun, 24 & 25 Dec   museudoazulejo.pt

Ceramic tiles, or *azulejos*, are a distinctive aspect of Portuguese culture. The National Tile Museum is enjoyable both for its excellent displays and beautiful setting: a 16th-century convent transformed over the centuries with Moorish tile displays from the 15th century right through to the present day.

1 Madre de Deus Church

The magnificent barrel-vaulted convent church, packed with paintings, is the result of three centuries of construction and opulent decoration. Its layout dates from the 16th century; the tile panels and gilt woodwork were added in the 17th- and 18th-century. The Museu Nacional do Azulejo is housed in this historic building.

2 Manueline Cloister

This small but stunning cloister is one of the few surviving features of the original convent of Madre de Deus. This is the Manueline style at its most restrained. The 17th-century geometrical wall tiles were added later in the 19th century.

3 Nossa Senhora da Vida Altarpiece

Almost 5 m (16 ft) square and containing over 1,000 tiles, this 16th-century Renaissance altarpiece is the work of João de Góis. It depicts the *Adoration of the Shepherds*, flanked by St Luke and St John.

4 Renaissance Cloister

Part of the first major alteration to the convent in the 16th century, this airy, two-level cloister is the work

 VIEW
Set around a central courtyard, the cloister is a serene spot, with its delicate columns and intricately carved walkways.

Madre de Deus Church's gilded Rococo altarpiece

of Diogo de Torralva. Glassed in to protect visitors and the collection from the weather, it is the light heart of the building.

5 Tile-Making Exhibit

Step-by-step exhibits on tile-making, from a lump of clay to final glazing, illuminate how the medium combines the practical and decorative.

6 Temporary Exhibitions

The ground and first floors have temporary exhibitions on subjects like contemporary tile art, an important art form in Portugal.

7 Shop

Numerous quality reproductions of classic tile designs are available at the museum's shop, as well as modern tiles and other gifts.

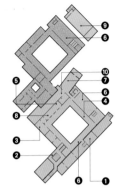

Museu Nacional do Azulejo Floorplan

Key to Floorplan

- Second floor
- First floor
- Ground floor

8 Moorish Tiles

With their attractive geometric patterns, varied colour palettes along with the glazing techniques, Moorish tiles continue to inspire tile-makers and home decorators alike.

9 Lisbon Panel

This vast tiled panorama of Lisbon, stretching 23 m (75 ft) in length, is a captivating depiction of the city's waterfront as it looked in about 1740, before the great earthquake. It was transferred here from one of the city's palaces.

10 Cafeteria and Winter Garden

Suitably tiled with food-related motifs, the museum cafeteria is a great stop for coffee or a light lunch. The courtyard is partly covered and forms a beautiful winter garden, providing a relaxed environment.

A NOD FROM THE 19TH CENTURY

When the southern façade of the church was restored in the late 19th century, the architect used as his model a painting now in the Museu de Arte Antiga (p28). This shows the convent and church as they looked in the early 16th century. Indoors, the quest for authenticity was less zealous. In one of the cloisters, 19th-century restorers have left a potent symbol of their own era: an image of a steam locomotive has been incorporated into one of the upper-level capitals.

A tiled *azulejo* panel showing a hunting scene

PALÁCIO NACIONAL DE QUELUZ

📍 A2 📍 Largo do Palácio 🕐 9am–6pm daily (gardens: to 6:30pm)
🚫 1 Jan & 25 Dec 🌐 parquesdesintra.pt 📱

Queluz is like a miniature Versailles – an exquisite Rococo palace with formal gardens and parkland, just 15 minutes from central Lisbon. The palace was initially intended as a summer residence but became the royal family's permanent home from 1794 until they moved to Brazil in 1807.

1 Robillion Pavilion

This impressive building, replete with exquisitely crafted windows, balustrades and pillars, is a bit too fussy for purists. It was designed by the famous French architect Robillion.

2 Gardens

A pair of formal gardens – the Hanging Garden and Malta Garden – occupy the space between the palace's two asymmetric wings. Laid out by Robillion, they are adorned with fountains, statues and topiary.

> **☕ DRINK**
> The terrace at the Pousada is the best place for a drink – unless you are lucky enough to have an invitation to the palace itself.

3 Cozinha Velha and Pousada Dona Maria I

The old palace kitchens have long housed the fine Cozinha Velha restaurant. A drink on the terrace of the newer Pousada Dona Maria I, in the former quarters of the Royal Guard, is as close as you'll get to living at Queluz.

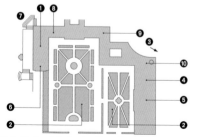

Palácio Nacional de Queluz Floorplan

The palace's ornate façade and formal gardens

4 Music Room

The Music Room was used for concerts and even opera performances, and doubled as a venue for important christenings. It still serves as a concert venue.

5 Throne Room

Competing in grandeur with the sumptuous Sala dos Embaixadores, the stunning dome-ceilinged Throne Room also served as the palace's ballroom, church and theatre.

6 Don Quixote Chamber

The circular-pattern floor and domed ceiling make this square room seem round. It is named for its painted scenes from *Don Quixote*.

7 Robillion Staircase

This beautiful staircase links the lower parkland to the palace. It is flanked by an arcaded gallery with a cascade flowing into a small lake; the royal family went boating here.

8 Sala dos Embaixadores

The magnificent Ambassadors' Room was used for diplomatic audiences, and is opulently decorated with stuccowork and painted and gilded carved woodwork. The *trompe l'oeil* ceiling depicts the royal family at such an event.

9 Corredor das Mangas

The hallway linking the old and newer parts of

Beautiful tile-work in the Corredor das Mangas

Queluz was named for the glass sleeves *(mangas)* of its candles. Painted wall tiles give it its other name, the *Corredor dos Azulejos*.

10 Chapel

The first room to be completed in 1752, the chapel also held concerts, some by Dona Maria I's own chamber orchestra. It is thought that she and her sisters painted some of the wall panels.

THE PIOUS QUEEN

Dona Maria I was the first undisputed Queen regnant of Portugal and the first monarch of Brazil. She was a noteworthy ruler but after her son died, she suffered with poor mental health. In 1807, she was exiled to Brazil to escape the invasion of Portugal led by the French Emperor Napoleon.

Lavish interior of the Sala dos Embaixadores

MUSEU CALOUSTE GULBENKIAN

⚲ F1 🏠 Avenida de Berna 45A 🕐 10am–6pm Wed–Mon 🚫 1 Jan, Easter Sun, 1 May, 24–25 Dec 🌐 gulbenkian.pt/museu ↗

Based on the private collections of Calouste Gulbenkian, the galleries here span over 4,000 years of art history. The museum is part of a complex that houses the Calouste Gulbenkian Foundation, a concert hall and auditoria, an art library and a park. The Foundation also features the CAM, a centre of modern and contemporary art.

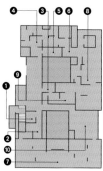

Museu Calouste Gulbenkian Floorplan

1 3rd Dynasty Egyptian Bowl

Found in a tomb north of Thebes, this elegant alabaster bowl was modelled on an every-day ointment bowl. The ancient Egyptians adorned tombs with copies of everyday objects made from noble materials. This one is 4,000 years old.

2 Ancient Greek Vase

This wide-rimmed terracotta vase (dating from the 5th century BCE) is decorated with various mythological motifs: the abduction of Phoebe and Hilaira, daughters of Leucippus, and a bacchanalian scene.

3 St Catherine and St Joseph

Two paintings by the 15th-century Flemish master Rogier van der Weyden are believed to be parts of an altar-piece; a third element is in London's National Gallery. The woman is thought to be Catherine of Alexandria.

4 Boy Blowing Bubbles

Édouard Manet's 1867 painting is not just a version of *Vanitas*, the popular allegory on the transience of life and art, but a deftly

Manet's Impressionist *Boy Blowing Bubbles*

painted portrait of Léon-Édouard Koëlla, stepson of the artist.

5 Lalique Collection

Gulbenkian was a close friend of the French Art Nouveau jeweller René Lalique and bought a great number of his beautiful pieces, many on show in this part of the museum.

6 Diana Statue

A graceful marble statue by the French sculptor Jean-Antoine Houdon, dating from 1780, is unusual for the era in that it depicts the goddess in move-ment, and completely naked. It belonged to Catherine the Great of Russia and was exhibited at the Hermitage, where its nudity caused quite a scandal.

7 Eastern Islamic Art

This large gallery displays a diverse collection of artifacts, such as manuscripts, carpets, textiles,

The Eastern Islamic Art gallery in the Museu Calouste Gulbenkian

ceramics and other objects from Turkey, Syria, the Caucasus (including Armenia), Persia and India.

8 Louis XV and XVI Furniture

Considered ostentatious by some, the ornate 18th-century French pieces in the decorative art collection fascinate for their materials and craftsmanship. Highlights include a magnificent Louis XV chest inlaid with lacquer

A finely crafted 18th-century table

TOP TIP

Explore temporary shows of Portuguese art in the Modern Collection.

panels, gold leaf, bronze, mother-of-pearl and ebony; and a table with a shelf that flips over to reveal a mirror.

9 Old Man With a Stick

This engaging *chiaroscuro* portrait of a bearded man is a wonderful example of Rembrandt's famous preoccupation with ageing. The gaze of the painting's subject is tired, and the large hands intricately lined. Nothing is known about the model.

10 Yuan Dynasty Stem Cup

This spectacularly crafted blue-glazed piece, dating from the beginning of the 14th century, is decorated with delicate reliefs of Taoist figures under bamboo leaves.

CALOUSTE GULBENKIAN

Gulbenkian (b 1869), who made his fortune by negotiating deals between oil companies, used his wealth to indulge his love of fine art. He came to Lisbon during World War II and lived here until his death in 1955. His will specified that a foundation be set up to look after his vast collection.

SINTRA

🏠 30 km (18 miles) NW of Lisbon Ⓦ cm-sintra.pt; parquesdesintra.pt

A UNESCO World Heritage Site, Sintra was the summer residence for Portuguese kings from the 13th century until Portugal became a republic in 1910. It still has the qualities of a hill retreat: a cool climate, greenery and a romantic atmosphere. The old town is pretty but crowded, while the surrounding landscapes and sights are a must visit.

1 Monserrate
A Moorish-style palace dominates the beautiful gardens of Monserrate, which were originally laid out by English residents.

THE ARTIST KING
Ferdinand Saxe-Coburg-Gotha was known as Dom Fernando II, the "artist" king. A lover of art, nature and new inventions of the time, the Dom was himself a painter. He commissioned the building of Palácio Nacional da Pena and lived there until his death in 1885.

2 Palácio Nacional da Pena
Dom Fernando II, Dona Maria II's German-born king consort, had this fabulous toyland palace built in the mid-19th century. The work of a lively imagination, it exhibits his eclectic tastes, and is preserved as it was when the royal family lived there. All visits to the palace must be booked in advance for a specific day and time.

3 Parque da Pena
The park around the Palácio da Pena is another of Dom Fernando II's contributions to Sintra's magic. It contains the chalet he had built for his second wife, Elise Hensler, an American opera singer.

4 Quinta da Regaleira
This lavish palace looms on a steep bend in the old road to Colares. It was built around 1900 for António Augusto Carvalho Monteiro, a millionaire and philanthropist who also owned Peninha (p104). Don't miss the inverted initiation well.

5 Eléctrico de Sintra
This tram line connects Sintra with Praia das Maçãs. The journey takes about 45 minutes, passing through leafy countryside and coastal villages.

Palácio Nacional da Pena
perched high above Sintra

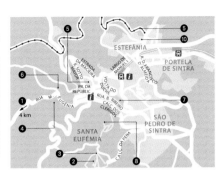

EAT
Try local treats such as *queijadas* (cheese tarts) at Queijadas da Sapa (*Volta do Duche 12*) and Casa Piriquita (*Rua Padarias 1*).

6 Palácio de Seteais

Built in 1787, Palácio de Seteais (*p117*) got its Neo-Classical façade later. It has now been transformed into a hotel and it's best to visit well dressed, for tea or a meal.

7 Parque da Liberdade

The picturesque town park, with its steep paths running among the trees, occupies the green valley below the old town.

8 Castelo dos Mouros

This 8th-century castle was captured by Afonso Henriques in 1147. Dom Fernando II partially rebuilt it in the 19th century. A chapel, with an exhibition about the castle's history, and a Moorish cistern are inside.

9 Palácio Nacional de Sintra

Twin conical chimneys mark the former royal palace. Begun in the 14th century and extended in the 16th, it is a captivating mix of styles from Moorish to Renaissance.

10 Centro Cultural Olga Cadaval

Sintra's main cultural venue, a modern centre hosting dance, theatre, concerts and films, was built in 1987, after a fire destroyed much of the Carlos Manuel cinema.

Clockwise from right
Ramparts of the Castelo dos Mouros; the Moorish-style dome of Monserrate; admiring the exhibits in the chapel at Castelo dos Mouros

TOP 10 OF EVERYTHING

Tilework at Mosteiro dos Jerónimos

MUSEUMS AND GALLERIES

1 Museu Nacional do Azulejo

Housed in a stunning convent and church, Lisbon's popular *azulejo* museum (p34) covers tiles and tile-making comprehensively, and has a pleasant café-restaurant.

2 MAAT – Museu de Arte, Arquitetura e Tecnologia

📍 B6 🏛 Avenida de Brasília
🕐 10am–7pm Wed–Mon 🌐 maat.pt

The stylish MAAT is dedicated to contemporary art, primarily Portuguese, along with modern architecture and technology.

3 Galeria 111

📍 C2 🏛 Rua Dr. João Soares 5B
🕐 10am–7pm Tue–Sat 🌐 111.pt

Since opening in 1964, this uptown contemporary art gallery has exhibited Portuguese artists, such as Paula Rego, Júlio Pomar and Joana Vasconcelos, as well as international artists.

4 Museu Calouste Gulbenkian

The Armenian oil baron and art collector Calouste Gulbenkian could well be the most important person in Lisbon postwar cultural life. His museum (p38) is a rare treat, not just because it covers so much in such a manageable way, but also because it has pleasant gardens and a good contemporary arts centre on site.

5 Zé dos Bois

📍 K4 🏛 Rua da Barroca 59
🕐 6–10pm Mon–Sat; Bar: 6pm–2am Mon–Thu (to 3am Fri & Sat)
🌐 zedosbois.org

ZDB, as it is also known, has consistently been Lisbon's most inspirational and genuinely "alternative" gallery. It is also a bar and a concert venue.

6 Museu Nacional de Arte Contemporânea do Chiado (MNAC)

Guardian of Portuguese modernity in art, this museum (p82) has a collection extending from the mid-19th century to the 21st century, though the decades after 1950 are less fully covered. There are also temporary exhibitions.

7 Museu Nacional dos Coches

You might not think of visit a coach museum if you didn't have a special interest in the subject. But this (p92) is one of Lisbon's most popular museums, thanks to its collection of 68 horse-drawn coaches and the connections they create with the past.

Exhibit at the Museu Nacional dos Coches

Paintings and at the Museu Nacional de Arte Antiga

8 Museu Nacional de Arte Antiga

Portugal's national museum *(p28)* houses priceless national and inter-national works, including painting, sculpture, textiles and decorative art. It is some-times called the Museu das Janelas Verdes due to the building's location in Rua das Janelas Verdes as well as its green windows.

9 Lisbon Story Centre

🅖 N5 🅐 Praça do Comércio 78–81 🕙 10am–7pm daily (last adm: 6pm) 🅦 lisboastory centre.pt

The centre offers a romp through Lisbon's history, presented in a series of rooms. Each period of time is recreated through models, paintings and multimedia displays, including a 4D version of the 1755 earthquake.

10 Fundação/Museu Arpad Szenes-Vieira da Silva

🅖 Praça das Amoreiras 56 🕙 10am–6pm Tue–Sun 🅦 fasvs.pt 🅯

Set in a former silk factory, this museum is devoted to the work of the 20th-century Portuguese modern-ist artist Maria Helena Vieira da Silva and her husband, the Hungarian painter Arpad Szenes.

TOP 10 PORTUGUESE ARTISTS

1. Nuno Gonçalves
Gonçalves is believed to be the 15th-century painter of *The Panels of St Vincent*, which may contain his self-portrait.

2. Vhils
Alexandre Farto (b 1987), better known as Vhils, is a famous Portugese street artist, known for his carved wall portraits.

3. Josefa de Óbidos
The work of this female painter and engraver (1630–84) falls between the Mannerist and the Baroque styles.

4. Graça Morais
This celebrated visual artist (b 1948) is known for her intense portraits and rural landscapes, some of which are featured at the Gulbenkian.

5. José Malhoa
A naturalistic painter (1855–1933) most famous for creating *O Fado*.

6. Columbano Bordalo Pinheiro
A gifted realist painter and portraitist, Columbano (1857–1929) painted many of the leading figures of the Republican movement.

7. Júlio Pomar
One of Portugal's most important 20th-century painters, Pomar (1926–2018) was at odds with the Fascist dictatorship.

8. Paula Rego
Portugal-born Rego (1935–2022) is known for producing prints and paintings based on children's books and Portuguese folk stories.

9. João Cutileiro
Born in Lisbon, this Portuguese sculptor (1937–2020) was renowned for his marble works depicting women's torsos.

10. Joana Vasconcelos
Feminist artist Vasconcelos (b 1971) subverts mundane objects, taking them out of their everyday context and transforming them into beautiful sculptures and large-scale install-ations. Examples include *Valkyrie Mumbet* and *Trafaria Praia*.

CHURCHES AND MONASTERIES

1 Mosteiro dos Jerónimos
The country's most significant monument (p24) displays the exuberant and Islamic-inspired ornamentation that is a chief characteristic of the Manueline style.

2 Sé de Lisboa
Seen at a distance, Lisbon's cathedral (p26) can almost conjure up the mosque that preceded it. Up close, the Romanesque building is attractively simple.

3 Igreja de São Domingos
One of Lisbon's oldest churches (p73) is one of its hardiest survivors. Built in 1242, it was damaged in the earthquakes of 1531 and 1755, and ravaged by fire in 1959. The church was also the seat of the Inquisition, and outside you'll find a modern memorial honouring the Jewish people killed during this period of history.

4 Basílica da Estrela
🗺 E4 🏛 Praça da Estrela 📞 213 960 915 🕐 Hours vary, call ahead
This landmark was built from 1779 to give thanks for the birth of a male heir to Dona Maria I. Sadly, the boy died of smallpox before the church was finished. Inside is the queen's tomb, and a nativity scene with over 500 cork-and-terracotta figures; ask the sacristan to show it to you.

5 Panteão Nacional
An unmistakable feature of the city's eastern skyline, this Baroque beauty (p68) is famous for having taken 284 years to complete. Built on a Greek cross plan with rounded arms, the church has similarities to St Peter's Basilica in Rome, although this church is even-sided. Otherwise known as Igreja de Santa Engrácia, the National Pantheon houses cenotaphs to Portuguese notables, including the writer Almeida Garrett and the *fado* singer Amália Rodrigues.

6 São Vicente de Fora
🗺 Q3 🏛 Largo de São Vicente 3 🕐 Church: 9am–1pm, 2:30–5pm Tue–Sun (to noon Sun); monastery: 10am–6pm Tue–Sun 🚻
In 1173, when St Vincent was proclaimed patron saint of Portugal, his relics were moved from the Algarve to the original church on this site. Philip II of Spain had the present Mannerist church built in the early 1600s. In 1885 the refectory was turned into the pantheon of the Bragança royal family.

7 Igreja da Graça
🗺 P2 🏛 Largo da Graça 🕐 9am–12:30pm & 2–5pm daily (to 7pm Sat & Sun)
This 1271 Augustinian monastery, rebuilt after the 1755 earthquake, is home to the Senhor dos Passos, a figure of Christ bearing the cross.

Ornate interior of the Basílica da Estrela

**The delicate pillars and arcades
of the Gothic Igreja do Carmo**

8 Igreja do Carmo
The late 14th-century church and convent of Carmo was one of Lisbon's main places of worship before the roof caved in on All Saints' Day 1755, killing the congregation. The evocative ruin, with its bare Gothic arches, now houses an archaeological museum (p83).

9 Igreja de São Roque
Built in the 16th century for the Jesuit order, this church (p81) is famous for its opulent interior, with gold leaf covering the beautiful carved detail, particularly the Chapel of St John the Baptist. Assembled in Rome, in the 1740s, using the most precious material available at that time, including lapis lazuli, agate, alabaster, amethyst, priceless marbles, gold and silver, the chapel was blessed by the pope, then taken apart and sent to Lisbon in three ships.

10 Igreja de Santo António
🗺 N4 🏠 Largo de Santo António da Sé 🕐 8am–7pm daily (to 8pm Sat & Sun)
Lisbon's most popular saint was allegedly born here (as Fernando Bulhões) in the late 12th century. The present Baroque church replaced the one lost to the 1755 earthquake. Weddings are held here in June – it's thought that St Anthony brings luck to newlyweds.

TOP 10 MANUELINE GEMS

1. Jerónimos Cloister
Belém's most popular tourist attraction, João de Castilho's cloister (p25) has the entire arsenal of Manueline features. Take your time here.

2. Torre de Belém
More decorative than defensive today, this tower (p32) is a perfect example of the Manueline style.

3. South Portal of Jerónimos
This riot of decoration – featuring saints, royals and other symbols – is completely symmetrical (p24).

4. Nave of Jerónimos
Mixing organic elements with geometry, octagonal piers encrusted with carvings rise up to the web-like vaulting (p24).

5. Conceição Velha Portal
Conceição Velha (p74) is the only remnant of the original 16th-century church, which was destroyed in the 1755 earthquake.

6. Portal, Museu do Azulejo
The portal of the museum (p34) dates from the 19th century, when the façade was reconstructed from a 16th-century painting.

7. Manueline Cloister, Museu do Azulejo
The small and restrained cloister (p34) is a reminder of the building's 16th-century role as a convent.

8. Ermida de São Jerónimo
A simple chapel (Rua Pero da Covilhã) from 1514 gives the Manueline a broader, more contemporary aesthetic.

9. Casa dos Bicos
This 16th-century palace combines Italian-style architecture with Manueline windows. It houses the José Saramago Foundation (josesaramago.org).

10. Rossio Station
Situated in the Baixa district, this station (p76) has a nostalgic Neo-Manueline look, which dates back to 1892, with a hint of Art Nouveau influence.

CITY VIEWS

1 Castelo de São Jorge
N3

The view from under the umbrella pines on the castle's esplanade takes in Alfama, the Baixa, Bairro Alto on the hill opposite, and the river. The light here is particularly appealing in the late afternoon. It is also a great spot to watch the sun set.

2 Miradouro de Santa Luzia
P4

This romantic viewpoint by the church of Santa Luzia has a pergola with tiled pillars, walls and benches. The veranda has dazzling vistas over the Alfama and across the river, a view shared by the adjacent café.

3 Miradouro de São Pedro de Alcântara
P4

This small garden is one of Lisbon's best-known viewpoints. Bougainvillea tumbles onto the next terrace, a formal and less accessible garden. The view extends across Restauradores and the Baixa to the Sé de Lisboa and the castle.

4 Miradouro de Santa Catarina
J5

Not just a visual vantage point, this is also a place to meet and hang out. A sculpture of Adamastor, the mythical creature from Camões' epic poem *The Lusiads*, presides over events from a stone plinth. There's a wide view of the river, encompassing the station at Cais do Sodré, the Alcântara docks and the 25 de Abril bridge.

5 Parque Eduardo VII

This park *(p95)* is not the most popular, thanks to its formal plan, steep incline and lack of shade. But climb to the top and the architect's

Parque Eduardo VII, the city's most iconic green space

Lisbon's picturesque skyline illuminated at sunset

the castle, the Graça church and the Mouraria quarter, as well as the Tejo estuary, the lower city, midtown Lisbon and the Monsanto park.

9 Jardim do Torel
□ L1

A less well known viewpoint, the Jardim do Torel is a small garden on a slope overlooking Restauradores and the Avenida da Liberdade. In summer, a pool is often installed here along with some sand to create a child-friendly urban beach.

10 Arco da Rua Augusta
□ M5

This impressively ornate arch dominates the north side of Praça do Comércio. It was built as a gateway to the reconstructed city following the 1755 earthquake, with the statues at the top representing Portuguese figures from history. Take a lift and a narrow spiral staircase to the top of the arch for stunning views over down-town Baixa. On the way back, you can visit the Clock Room, an exhibition space alongside the workings of the original 19th-century clock.

plan makes sense, as Lisbon stretches away from you in an unbroken perspective right down to the river. The sides of the park have a less commanding view but offer more shade. At the end of summer, bookworms gather here for the Feira do Livro, Lisbon's annual book fair.

6 Elevador de Santa Justa

The best close-up overview of the Baixa and Rossio, with the castle looming above, is to be had from the terrace at the top of the Elevador de Santa Justa (p75). It is reached via an extremely tight spiral staircase, but the view is definitely worth the climb.

7 Igreja da Graça
□ P2

The pine-shaded esplanade by the Graça church has a café with a classic view of the lower city, the river and the bridge. Like the castle's viewpoint, this one is best visited in the late afternoon.

8 Miradouro da Senhora do Monte
□ P1

One of the highest vantage points in the city, Our Lady of the Mount (there is a small chapel behind the viewpoint) affords a grand vista that encompasses

BEACHES

1 Caparica Norte
South of Lisbon, the scenic Caparica coast is busiest at its northern end, where you'll find Caparica town, plus an assortment of mid-range hotels, holiday homes, campsites and restaurants.

2 Carcavelos
The broadest and longest beach along the Estoril coast is far enough from Lisbon for clean water and yet close enough for an afternoon outing. Beachside bars and restaurants provide ample opportunity for meals and refreshments. This is an excellent surfing area, and there are a number of surf schools at the beach. Carcavelos is still extremely pleasant out of season.

3 Sesimbra
Located 45 minutes from Lisbon, the small fishing town of Sesimbra is sheltered at the foot of the Arrábida mountains. The town has a long beach, divided by a handsome fort, ideal for families seeking calm crystalline waters. Perched atop a pine-covered hill, a castle overlooks the town, adding to its charm. Sesimbra is also popular for its seafood reastuarants. For transport, local buses depart from a stand opposite Lisbon zoo.

4 Estoril and Cascais
These beaches get very crowded, as they are mostly short and narrow.

Still, the promenade that runs just above them, all the way from Estoril to Cascais, is full of relaxed bars and restaurants, where you can also take in the sun.

5 Adraga
Beyond Cabo da Roca, this pretty beach is reached via Almoçageme, off the Sintra road. Sintra's cooler climate prevails in this area. There's just one restaurant, but it is excellent.

6 Guincho
Guincho can provide an eyeful of sand on a windy day, but experienced surfers love it and it is the least developed of all the beaches along the Cascais coast. Beyond the built-up outskirts of Cascais, and with the Sintra hills as a backdrop, Guincho is a magnificent spot, and it draws the crowds on summer weekends. To avoid parking hassles, rent a bicycle in Cascais and ride out on the track that runs alongside the spectacular coast road.

7 Praia Grande, Sintra
With the longest unbroken stretch of sand in the area, Grande is popular with surfers and bodyboarders. There are also plenty of bars and restaurants, and one hotel.

Lagoa de Albufeira, a popular kitesurfing spot

8 Lagoa de Albufeira and Meco

The southern half of the Caparica coast is accessible only by driving towards Sesimbra. Lagoa de Albufeira is a lagoon popular with kitesurfers. Further south, Meco is backed by a village with restaurants and bars.

9 Praia das Maçãs

"Apple Beach" is one of the most family-friendly beaches along the Sintra-Colares coast. It has a picnic area, a playground and swimming pools complete with slides. There are lots of good seafood restaurants nearby, too.

10 Praia da Ursa

Not marked on maps and requiring a steep walk on narrow paths, Ursa is one of the most secluded beaches in the region. Surrounded by towering cliffs, it has no amenities or lifeguards and the waves can be powerful. The beach is reached along the road to Cabo da Roca, where there is a small sign marked Ursa to designate the parking area.

The beach and promenade along the coast at Estoril

TOP 10
OUTDOOR ACTIVITIES

1. Mountain Biking
Lisbon's hills provide ideal terrain for mountain biking. For country biking, head to the tracks around Sintra or Arrábida.

2. Cycling
Cycling is becoming increasingly popular in Lisbon, and bikes can be rented in Cascais and near Belém.

3. Board Sports
Surfing and bodyboarding are big along the Estoril and Sintra coasts, as is kitesurfing on the Caparica coast.

4. Fishing
Fishers seem to be all along the river and beaches. Tourists hoping to cast out a line can take organized boat trips off the coast of Cascais.

5. Bird-watching
The Tagus marshlands beyond Alcochete and the Tróia peninsula are rich in bird life almost all year round.

6. Sailing
There are sailing schools in Parque das Nações, Belém and along the Cascais coast. Renting larger craft is possible.

7. Horse Riding
There are a number of *equestre* or *hípico* clubs around Cascais and Sintra, and around Campo Grande in Lisbon.

8. Jogging
The western riverfront is ideal jogging territory, as is Parque Eduardo VII. Monsanto and the Guincho coast are other options.

9. Walking
Many quiet walks can be found in beautiful Sintra, Arrábida or the area surrounding the Tejo estuary.

10. Roller Skating
Parque das Nações, the Alcântara docks and Belém all have areas suitable for skating.

OFF THE BEATEN TRACK

1 Cristo Rei
📍 Almada ⏰ 10am–7pm daily (Oct–Mar: to 6pm) 🌐 cristorei.pt

From his perch on the south side of the river, Christ the King overlooks Lisbon. The 28-m (92-ft) statue on its 82-m (270-ft) pedestal was inaugurated in 1959, in thanks for Portugal's escape from involvement in World War II. Inspired by the famous statue in Rio de Janeiro, it has since become an important site of pilgrimage. Lifts ascend to the platform at the foot of the statue.

2 Prazeres
📍 D4 🚃 Praça São João Bosco ⏰ 9am–5:30pm daily (Oct–Apr: to 4:30pm) 🌐 cm-lisboa.pt

Take tram 28 to the end of the line to visit Lisbon's main cemetery, a neatly laid-out village of pristine tombs. This tranquil spot is where some of Lisbon's most important inhabitants have been buried, among some of Iberia's oldest cypress trees.

3 Cacilhas
Enjoy a ferry ride from Cais do Sodré to this little port opposite Lisbon, which is home to some terrific fish restaurants, as well as the Dom Fernando II e Glória, a restored 19th-century frigate that is now a museum.

4 Lapa
📍 E5

Set on a steep hillside overlooking the Tejo (or Tagus, in English), Lapa is a desirable district lined with lavish villas and mansions occupied by embassies, consulates and the rich.

5 Praça das Amoreiras
📍 E3

Locals enjoy drinking coffee at a kiosk under the trees in this hidden-away square, complete with a children's play area. The space is flanked by the arches of the last stretches of the 18th-century Aqueduto das Águas Livres, which brought water to the capital.

6 Aqueduto das Águas Livres
If you have a head for heights, you can walk across the top of the most dramatic part of Lisbon's extraordinary aqueduct (p90). It was built over a decade before the 1755 earthquake – which it survived, continuing to supply water to a shattered city.

7 Palácio das Necessidades
📍 D5 🚃 Largo das Necessidades ⏰ Gardens: 8am–8pm Mon–Fri, 10am–7pm Sat & Sun (Oct–Mar: to 6pm) 🌐 informacoeseservicos.lisboa.pt

This pink-hued 18th-century palace was built by Dom João V and used by Portuguese royals until 1910. It now belongs to the Foreign Ministry. The interior is closed to the public, but the gardens are delightful.

Crypts and tombs in Prazeres, the main cemetery of Lisbon

Vibrant cobbled street in LX Factory

8 LX Factory
🗺 D6 🏠 R. Rodrigues de Faria 103 🕙 Hours vary, chech website 🌐 lxfactory.com

This former factory complex is now a hipster enclave packed with bars, restaurants, boutiques and galleries. Don't miss Livraria Ler Devagar, a photo-worthy bookstore with a large English language section and a cosy café bar.

9 Poço dos Negros Area
🗺 F4 🏠 Rua do Poço dos Negros, Rua de São Bento, Rua dos Poiais de São Bento

Located between Estrela and Bairro Alto, this area has become one of Lisbon's creative hotspots (p59). Here you'll find grocery shops such as Mercearia Poço dos Negros alongside modern design stores and trendy cafés such as The Mill and Hello, Kristoff.

10 Barbadinhos Steam Pumping Station
🗺 P2 🏠 Rua do Alviela 12 🕙 10am–12:30pm & 1:30–5:30pm Tue–Sun 🌐 epal.pt

This fascinating relic of Victorian ingenuity was built in 1880 to pump water from a nearby reservoir up Lisbon's steep hills. The station worked non-stop until 1928. It is now a museum, which houses the former steam machines. Particularly interesting is the exhibit on the 17th-century Chafariz d'El Reione, one of Lisbon's first fountains. The museum also hosts temporary exhibits.

FAMILY ATTRACTIONS

1 Oceanário de Lisboa
Opened for the 1998 Lisbon Expo, the Oceanário de Lisboa *(p30)* remains the biggest single attraction in Parque das Nações. One of Europe's biggest aquariums, it holds an impressive array of species.

2 Roller Skating, Ice Skating and Skateboarding
There are several places in Lisbon with ramps and rinks for roller skating and skateboarding. One of the best is by the Vasco da Gama bridge in Parque das Nações *(p30)*. In winter, an outdoor ice rink is erected in Parque Eduardo VII *(p95)*.

3 Pavilhão do Conhecimento - Ciência Viva
This hands-on science museum *(p31)* has intriguing gadgetry to illustrate the fundamental laws of nature, including a bicycle ride on a 6-m- (20-ft-) high wire. Downstairs, the youngest visitors get the chance to don hard hats and help build the Unfinished House.

4 Quake
🗺 B6 🏛 Rua Cais de Alfândega Velha 39 🕐 Entry at specific time slots between 10am and 7pm; book ahead via website 🌐 lisbon quake.com

Experience Lisbon's 1755 earthquake at this interactive museum, complete with simulators. Children under four are not admitted.

5 Monsanto
🗺 B2

Monsanto *(p90)* is a pine wood located on the city's western fringes. The Parque Recreativo do Alto da Serafina and Parque Infantil do Alvito are both popular, fenced-off, well-equipped play areas.

6 Swimming Pools
Many hotels have outdoor pools. The Clube Nacional de Natação has a complex with indoor and outdoor pools at Rua de São Bento 209, or try the Piscina do Oriente at Rua Câmara Reis in east Lisbon.

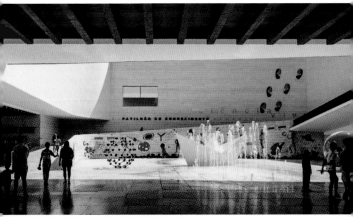

Interactive exhibits at the Pavilhão do Conhecimento - Ciência Viva

Spiral initiation well in Quinta da Regaleira

7 Quinta da Regaleira

Underground tunnels, spiral staircases and hidden tree paths make this 20th-century estate (p40) a fun maze to explore for kids and adults alike. Follow the steps down the initiation well and don't miss the stepping stones over the water stream. Bring a flashlight as some passages can get pretty dark.

8 Museu da Electricidade

🗺 B6 🏠 Avenida de Brasilia
🕐 10am–7pm Wed–Mon

Located on Lisbon's waterfront, the Electricity Museum, which is a part of the MAAT (p44), includes a section where children can play and learn.

9 Beaches

The Atlantic is not the safest for young ones to play in. Low tide is an advisable time for building sand castles and paddling in pools left by the receding sea. Some of the beaches along the Cascais coast (p61) are more protected; alternatively head for the calm waters of Sesimbra (p50), Arrábida or Tróia (p62).

10 Museu Nacional de História Natural e da Ciência

🗺 J2 🏠 Rua da Escola Politécnica 58
🕐 10am–5pm Tue–Sun (Gardens: to 8pm in summer)

Housed in the grand setting of the old Polytechnic, this science and natural history museum by the Jardim Botânico (p88) has an engaging exhibit illustrating the basic principles of physics.

TOP 10 FAMILY-FRIENDLY RESTAURANTS

1. Nosolo Itália
A tempting array of pizzas, pastas and ice creams are served on a large outdoor terrace (p93).

2. Mercado da Ribeira
🏠 Avenida 24 de Julho
🌐 timeoutmarket.com
This massive food hall features over 40 dining options.

3. Casanova
A popular quay-side pizzeria (p71) with a safe veranda; kids can watch the chef at work.

4. Café Buenos Aires
🏠 Calçada do Duque 31B
🌐 cafebuenosaires.pt
The steps outside are traffic-free; inside, the vibe is friendly.

5. Psi
The pretty gardens surrounding this restaurant (p99) are perfect for children to play in.

6. Chapitô a Mesa
🏠 Costa do Castelo 7 ☎ 218 875 077
Part of a popular circus school, this restaurant offers amazing views and a delightful menu.

7. Verjus Bar à Vins
🗺 E4 🏠 Rua da Trinas 67A
☎ 211 947 477
This family-friendly space offers a playground and a restaurant with a kids' menu.

8. Restaurants at Doca de Santo Amaro
🏠 Doca de Santo Amaro
Facing a marina, these family-friendly restaurants have outdoor tables.

9. Restaurants in Parque das Nações
🏠 Parque das Nações
Choices here range from food courts to riverside terraces and steak houses.

10. Restaurants along Rua Vieira Portuense, Belém
This is a short street of outdoor restaurants overlooking the Jardim Botânico de Belém (p88).

BARS AND NIGHTCLUBS

1 Lisboa Rio
📍 K6 🏠 Cais Gás 7

This Mediterranean restaurant and bar, with a beautiful terrace overlooking the dock, transforms into a swanky night-club at weekends. With both resident and guest DJs from all over the world, there is lively music and entertainment.

2 Cais do Gás
📍 F5 🌐 caisdogas.com

Old warehouses along Lisbon's riverfront have been converted into bars and clubs. Classics like Jamaica and Tokyo moved here from Pink Street, joining others like Titanic Sur Mer, with its live acts, and B.Leza, famous for its afro tunes.

3 Fábrica Braço de Prata
📍 C2 🏠 Rua Fábrica de Material de Guerra 1

A former ammunitions factory on the eastern side of town, Fábrica Braço de Prata is now a hip cultural centre. It provides live music, theatre and a chance to dance with fleet-footed locals at fortnightly *forró* sessions.

4 Lux
📍 R3 🏠 Cais da Pedra, Avenida Infante Dom Henrique

Located by the harbour and housed in a former warehouse, Lux is considered Lisbon's most stylish and varied night-club. With a downstairs dance floor, an upstairs bar and dance area, a rooftop terrace, retro decor and a string of hot DJs, it lives up to the hype.

5 Bar Lounge
📍 J5 🏠 Rua da Moeda 1

Resident disc-spinner Mário Valente has been working to enrich Bar Lounge's eclectic mix of indie and electronic pop and rock since the early noughties. Located down an alley, this place has a full programme of live bands that, combined with a relaxed atmosphere, has earned it a loyal following.

6 Damas
📍 P2 🏠 Rua da Voz do Operário 60

This nightlife institution in lively Graça hosts local DJs and live bands after dark. It's a mixed musical bag, so enjoy the set being played and arrive early to beat the queues.

7 Incógnito
📍 F4 🏠 Rua dos Poiais de São Bento 37

This veteran of the early 1990s has kept on doing what it does best and draws a mostly low-profile crowd. Somewhere between a bar and a club, it accommodates both chill-out areas and a dance floor. DJs spin indie tracks with a dash of techno, disco and post-punk.

8 Ministerium
📍 G5 🏠 Terreiro do Paço, Ala Nascente 72–73

This stylish waterfront nightclub, with a large dance floor and bar, has one of

Colourful umbrellas above Rua Nova do Carvalho (Pink Street)

the best locations in town, plus music from big-name local and international DJs. Crowds begin to gather post-midnight for DJ sets, which veer towards techno and electronica. Many events continue until dawn.

9 Park Rooftop

📍 N5 📍 Calçada do Combro 58
🕐 Sun

Hidden above a multistorey car park, this slick rooftop bar is popular among Lisbon's young crowd. It offers great sunset views, tasty cocktails and late-night DJs. Unlike many Lisbon rooftop bars, it's open year-round.

10 Rua Nova do Carvalho (Pink Street)

📍 K6

Once the sort of street to avoid after dark, this has now been cleaned up and rebranded as "Pink Street", thanks to the alarming colour of the road. The result: one of the hippest streets in which to spend the evening. Old dance clubs such as Roterdão Club are still to be found, alongside trendy bars such as Povo, Collect Records and the club/music venue Musicbox.

TOP 10
FADO VENUES

1. Parreirinha de Alfama
📍 Beco do Espírito Santo 1
🌐 parreirinhadealfama.com
A traditional venue set up by the famous singer Argentina Santos.

2. Clube de Fado
📍 Rua de São João da Praça 94
🌐 clubedefado.pt
This Alfama *fado* venue hosts *fadistas* like Maria Ana Bobone.

3. Senhor Vinho
📍 Rua do Meio à Lapa 18
🌐 srvinho.com/en
Quality and style characterize the singing at this expensive restaurant.

4. Maria da Mouraria
📍 Largo da Severa 2 🌐 mariada mouraria.eatbu.com
High-quality *fado* in the former home of celebrated *fadista* Maria Severa.

5. Tasca do Chico
📍 Rua do Diário de Notícias 39
📞 961 339 696
The place to see gritty *fado vadio*: amateur impromptu performances.

6. Café Luso
📍 Travessa da Queimada 10
🌐 cafeluso.pt/en
Offering first-class *fado* and fine food in the Bairro Alto since the 1920s.

7. Sr Fado
📍 Rua dos Remédios 176
🌐 sr-fado.com
Warm and friendly venue with some of the best *fado* performers in town.

8. A Severa
📍 Rua das Gáveas 51
🌐 asevera.com/en
An atmospheric venue named after the famous 19th-century *fadista*.

9. Fado em Si
📍 Rua de São João da Praça 18
🌐 fadoemsi.com
Choices range from food courts to riverside terraces and steak houses.

10. O Faia
📍 Rua da Barroca 54
🌐 ofaia.com
One of Bairro Alto's larger venues, with good music and expensive food.

SHOPPING DISTRICTS

1 Avenida da Liberdade
⌘ F3

Lisbon's main avenue, rising from the Baixa to the Parque Eduardo VII, has become the country's prime slice of real estate. It is lined with shops owned by upmarket designer brands, including Cartier, Gucci, Armani, Hugo Boss and Prada.

2 Chiado
⌘ L4

Traditionally the quarter with Lisbon's most elegant shops, the Chiado is now the city's most varied shopping area. It mixes quiet streets with lively squares and sheet-music suppliers with street-cred fashion boutiques.

3 Avenidas Guerra Junqueiro/Roma
⌘ G1

Head to Avenida Guerra Junqueiro and adjacent Avenida de Roma for good clothing stores and cafés – and pay a visit to the Museu Rafael Bordalo Pinheiro (p98). There's also a shopping complex nearby with several boutiques and delicatessens.

4 Baixa
⌘ M4–5

The charm of the Baixa lies with its courteous shopkeepers, some of whom still stand behind wooden counters and do sums on bits of paper. For all that, the pedestrianized Rua Augusta is lined with modern chains.

5 Campo de Ourique/ Amoreiras
⌘ E3

Gentrification proceeds at a gentle pace in Campo de Ourique. The grid street plan makes for lots of corner bakeries, cafés and small shops. Nearby, the brash Amoreiras Shopping Centre, the first of its kind in Lisbon, has high street favourites.

6 Rua de São Bento/ Príncipe Real
⌘ F4

Rua de São Bento is a mini-district specializing in antiques and second-hand shops. It's a short hop to pleasant Praça das Flores for a coffee under the trees, and then an uphill walk to Príncipe Real, and a cluster of more expensive antiques shops.

7 Bairro Alto
⌘ K3–4

Like the big shopping centres, Bairro Alto offers night-time shopping, but in a much cooler setting, and with the option of sipping a drink as you shop. Some stores seem ineffably

Chic and vibrant clothes at a store in Bairro Alto

trendy, but Bairro Alto is a hub for Portuguese fashion and design.

8 Fresh Food Markets
🗺 K6, E3, F2

Prices at Lisbon's food markets may not be lower than in the supermarkets, but the produce is often fresher and the experience is much more rewarding. Among the best are Mercado da Ribeira, opposite Cais do Sodré station; Mercado de Campo de Ourique, in west Lisbon; and Mercado 31 de Janeiro, opposite the DoubleTree by Hilton hotel on Rua Engenheiro Vieira da Silva.

9 Poço dos Negros Area
🗺 R3

Running along the 28 tram line, this is one of the city's creative corners (p53). Here local design shops and trendy cafés mix with traditional Portuguese restaurants and a tea store, which sells local blends such as the Lisbon Breakfast.

10 Feira da Ladra
🗺 Q2 🗺 Campo de Santa Clara 🕘 9am–6pm Tue & Sat

Lisbon's Thieves' Market sells quirky items such as beautiful brass taps that won't fit any known plumbing system. As with most flea markets, it's all about the sights and sounds, the people and the haggling.

Rua Augusta in Baixa lined with trendy shops

TOP 10 THINGS TO BUY

1. Ceramics
Portuguese ceramics extend from tiles to pottery, and from rustic to twee.

2. Embroidery
Bordados are delicate, but long-lasting, old-world table linen.

3. Cork items
Portugal is the world's biggest exporter of cork. Local artisans use this sustainable material to make a variety of objects, including wallets, umbrellas and shoes.

4. Shoes
Fewer shoes are made in Portugal these days, but are very high quality.

5. Tea
Discover unique local tea blends at the Companhia Portugueza do Chá.

6. Beauty Supplies
Find delightful-smelling soaps wrapped in stunning vintage-inspired packaging at Claus Porto.

7. Cheese
Choose from runny Serra ewe's milk cheeses, delicious Serpa and Azeitão, peppery Castelo Branco and excellent hard and soft goat's cheeses.

8. Hams and Smoked Meats
The best *presunto* (cured ham) is from the north, but the Alentejan ham of the Ibérico pig is arguably better. Taste first, and decide for yourself.

9. Preserved Foods
Sardines and other tinned fish, olives, olive oil, *massa de pimentão* (red-pepper paste) and chilli sauce are all superb and readily available.

10. Wine
A wisely spent €5 will get you a truly good wine; €20 an unforgettable one. The wide choice is a pleasant surprise.

A wine shop

LISBON FOR FREE

Popular flea market Feira da Ladra bustling with shoppers

1 Feira da Ladra
Lisbon's rambling flea market (p59) is as good for people-watching as it is for finding the odd bargain among a panoply of clothes, antiques and crafts. Arrive early to bag the most interesting items.

2 Museu do Dinheiro
📍 M5 🏠 Largo de S. Julião
🕙 10am–6pm Wed–Sun
🌐 museudodinheiro.pt

The Money Museum portrays the evolution of Portugal's various currencies over the centuries. One of the highlights of the museum is a rare portion of the city's original King Dinis Wall in the crypt of an old church.

3 Riverside Walk
📍 D6–A6

The riverside is largely traffic-free from the Doca de Santo Amaro to the Torre de Belém, making for a lovely stroll past the dramatic Ponte 25 de Abril and Belém's monuments.

4 Jardim Gulbenkian
The Calouste Gulbenkian's (p38) Modernist gardens offer a quiet respite from the city's bustle. Ducks paddle around the large central pond, while turtles hide in little streams. It's a favourite spot for residents who come here for a reading break, a family picnic, or to catch the latest exhibit at the museums nearby.

5 Núcleo Arqueológico da Rua dos Correeiros
Phone ahead to book a fascinating free guided tour that takes you below the Millennium BCP bank in Baixa (p73). Builders uncovered ancient remains here while working on the bank in the 1990s, and excavations have revealed Roman fish-preserving tanks, Moorish ceramics and Christian graves.

6 Jerónimos Church
The church of Santa Maria de Belém, built to commemorate Vasco da Gama's voyage to India over 500 years ago, is Portugal's most striking example of Manueline architecture and also an integral part of Mosteiro dos Jerónimos (p24). Slender pillars rise like palm trees to the spectacular vaulted roof in the church.

7 Festival for Santo António
🔲 H4 🏠 Alfama

On 12–13 June, Lisbon celebrates its main saint's day. There are free daytime parades and most districts have evening street parties with food stalls and dancing. The Alfama is the best place to head if you want to join in the festivities.

8 Jardim da Estrela
🔲 E4 🏠 Praça da Estrela

In the shadow of the basilica, the well-maintained Estrela Gardens in the western part of the city are very popular with locals. There's a small lake and a bandstand set in the middle of neat flower beds, statues and pleasant walkways. Visitors can also relax at the open-air cafés which offer various options for snacks.

9 Rua Augusta
The broad, pedestrianized main street (p73) through the Baixa usually offers plenty of free entertainment, from living statues to mime artists. Look out for the triumphal arch at the end of the street.

10 Cascais Coast
Lisbon is close to some fantastic stretches of beach. Head to Estoril and you can walk up the seafront promenade to Cascais (p101), past several sandy beaches.

The town of Estoril perched on the coast near Cascais

TOP 10
BUDGET TIPS

1. You can explore all of central Lisbon on foot. Make sure you have sturdy shoes to negotiate its many hills.

2. Do what the locals do and enjoy a cheaper dinner by having a picnic at the *miradouros* at sunset. Grab wine, snacks and a variety of food from Lisbon's inexpensive supermarkets.

3. The Bilhete Diário, a one-day travel pass (€10.70), allows unlimited access to buses, trains, the metro and trams. There is also a 24-hour train-and-metro pass (€6.60).

4. The Lisboa Card (€22 for one-day, €37 for two days, €46 for three days), available from tourist offices, allows free travel on public transport and admission to 39 major sights around the city.

5. Take the passenger ferry from Cais do Sodré to Cacilhas across the Tejo; it's a shorter ride than a boat trip, but the views are just as good.

6. Check for free festivals, concerts or events on the city's listings website (agendalx.pt).

7. Take advantage of the good-value set meals in cafés and restaurants.

8. It's normal to be offered an array of starters when you sit down in a restaurant, but you'll pay for anything you eat. Politely decline anything you don't want to have.

9. At the MAAT (p44), you can climb to the top of the museum's undulating rooftop for free and enjoy panoramic views overlooking the river.

10. There are inexpensive bike hire outfits on the riverfront at Belém and in Cascais; cycling is the best way to explore these relatively flat districts.

EXCURSIONS

Charming hilltop castle at Palmela wine country

1 Palmela and Azeitão

The main sight in Palmela is its hilltop castle, now an elegant *pousada*, which is open to passing visitors. Vila Fresca de Azeitão and Vila Nogueira de Azeitão are neighbouring towns at the heart of Palmela wine country.

2 Serra da Arrábida

This limestone massif, about 40 minutes south of Lisbon by car, provides Portugal with its Mediterranean-like scenery – calm, blue-green waters and dramatic cliffs. Head for Portinho da Arrábida, and stop frequently to admire the views as you get close.

3 Alcácer do Sal

The ancient town of Alcácer do Sal (*al-kasr* from the Arabic for castle, and *do sal* from its trade in salt) sits peacefully on the north bank of the River Sado. Here you can enjoy the views from the 6th-century castle (now a *pousada*) and relax in the pleasant cafés along the riverside promenade.

4 Sintra Hills

The romantic beauty of Sintra (*p40*) and its palaces – the crumbling walls veiled with moss, the views, the winding roads under dense canopies of leaves – all combine to make a visit to the Sintra hills a magical experience.

5 Óbidos

Óbidos is arguably the most picturesque town in Portugal. Contained within the walls of a 14th-century castle, it is filled with whitewashed houses with their edges painted ochre or blue, and their windows adorned with lace curtains and potted geraniums. The town was the wedding gift of Dom Dinis to his queen, Isabel of Aragon, in 1282.

6 Tejo Estuary

Referred to in English as the Tagus, the estuary is accessible from Lisbon via Alcochete, just across the Vasco da Gama bridge. From here you can drive or walk into the Lezíria marshlands, one of Europe's most important staging sites for migrating water birds, including flamingo, black-tailed godwit and avocet.

7 Setúbal and Tróia

The port town of Setúbal is prosaic, but it is home to the Igreja de Jesus, the first and perhaps most distinctive example of the Manueline style. People and cars are ferried across the mouth of the Sado river to the Tróia peninsula, which has excellent beaches extending south, and its estuary side is a haven for birds.

Flamingoes taking to the sky at the Tróia peninsula

Stunning interior of the library at Mafra

8 Mafra

Mafra is home to an extravagant palace and monastery built for Dom João V, Portugal's 18th-century monarch, who had a weakness for excess of all kinds. The almost pyramidal proportions of its construction are entertainingly detailed in José Saramago's novel *Baltasar and Blimunda*. A section of Mafra's hunting grounds is now used for a wolf conservation project.

9 Tomar

The UNESCO-listed Convento do Cristo is the main attraction of this Templar town in Central Portugal. Founded by the Portuguese crusader Gualdim Pais in 1160, it follows the Manueline architecture style with its plateresque façades and marine motifs.

10 Ribatejo Wine Route

Some of the best wine producers in the Ribatejo region are clustered on the left bank of the Tejo, particularly between the towns of Almeirim and Alpiarça. Seek out Quinta do Casal Branco, Quinta da Alorna, Fiuza & Bright and Quinta da Lagoalva de Cima.

TOP 10
BEAUTY SPOTS

1. Monserrate
Designed in a romantic style with springs and fountains, the stunning gardens and palace-pavilion of Monserrate *(p102)* remain popular.

2. Castelo dos Mouros
The steeply stepped walls of this attractive 8th-century castle *(p41)* offer some really fabulous views.

3. Penedo
This village on the high road from Sintra to the coast is misty and romantic in winter and a cool refuge in summer.

4. Peninha
This small sanctuary *(p104)* offers views of Europe's western edge, plus a group of buildings with an intriguing history.

5. Praia da Ursa
Stroll along this secluded beach *(p51)*, enjoy the calm breeze and take in the sheer beauty of the place.

6. Guincho Coast
Cars drive very slowly – a rare thing in Portugal – along this beautifully scenic road *(p101)*, leading to the foot of the Sintra hills. Here is the superb Guincho beach, which is ideal for windsurfing and boardsurfing.

7. Portinho da Arrábida
One of the most protected beaches along the western seaboard looks as though it belongs in Croatia or Turkey.

8. Sesimbra
This pretty town *(p50)* has a plethora of seafood restaurants and pristine family-friendly beaches. There's also a picturesque coastline ideal for kayaking or boat tours.

9. Cabo Espichel
The clifftop southwesternmost point of the Setúbal peninsula is in some ways more attractive than the better known Cabo da Roca.

10. Bucelas and Beyond
Head here for a taste of inland Estremadura – and some superb white wine.

AREA BY AREA

Alfama district

ALFAMA, CASTELO AND THE EAST

Alfama's Arabic-sounding name recalls its past as an important district of Moorish Lisbon. No buildings survive from this era, but Alfama suffered little damage in the 1755 earthquake, so its medieval street plan has remained intact – and largely traffic-free. The Castelo neighbourhood at the top adjoins the higher hill district of Graça. To the south and east, Alfama descends to the river.

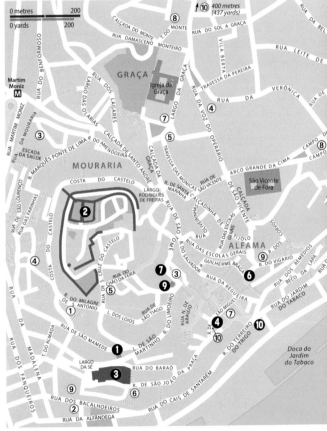

For places to stay in this area, see p114

1 Museu do Teatro Romano

📍 N4 📍 Rua São Mamede 3
🕐 10am–6pm Tue–Sun 🌐 museu
delisboa.pt/pt/nucleos 📷

A Roman amphitheatre dating from the 1st century BCE lies beneath the buildings just above the Sé de Lisboa. Excavations are ongoing but it seems to have been a sizable structure, seating up to 5,000. Visitors are offered an insight into the archaeological work that continues here, as well as at various other sites in central Lisbon.

Walking along the ramparts of the Castelo de São Jorge

2 Castelo de São Jorge

The castle that crowns Alfama was the heart of the city in the Moorish era, and the site (p22) goes back to Phoenician times at least. The picturesque residential area within the castle's outer walls is also called Castelo.

3 Sé de Lisboa

The English crusader Gilbert of Hastings, Lisbon's first bishop, oversaw the construction of the city's cathedral in the mid-12th century. The site (p26) was previously occupied by a mosque, parts of which have been excavated.

4 Largo de São Miguel

📍 P4

You can reach this square, located in the heart of Alfama, via steps from Largo das Portas do Sol; walk down next to Santa Luzia church and bear left after the first corner. This route captures the essence of Alfama: narrow alleys that older residents use as gardens, grills with sardines smoking, patios, archways and twisting stairs. The absence of cars lets children play everywhere. On 12 June every year, Largo de São Miguel is at the centre of the huge party thrown to honour St Anthony, Lisbon's most popular saint.

5 Igreja de Santa Engrácia/ Panteão Nacional

R3 **Campo de Santa Clara** **10am–6pm Tue–Sun (Oct–Mar: to 5pm)** **panteaonacional.gov.pt**

The soaring dome of Santa Engrácia is a landmark on Lisbon's low eastern skyline, but when you approach it on foot it seems to duck out of view at every turn. The dome was added in 1966 – 284 years after the construction of the church began. This in turn has enriched the Portuguese language with a saying that translates as "a job like Santa Engrácia", for any interminable project. The airy, marble-clad interior serves as the National Pantheon.

6 Santo Estevão

Q4

The small esplanade in front of the Santo Estevão church is one of the area's best viewing points. Access is easy, if steep, from Largo do Chafariz de Dentro, at the foot of Alfama, where you will find one of the city's oldest public fountains (as well as the Fado Museum, so you can easily combine a visit to both). Just head up Rua dos Remédios and climb the Escadinhas de Santo Estevão steps on your left.

7 Largo das Portas do Sol

P4

When the 28 tram gets to the top of the hill beyond the Sé de Lisboa, it squeezes between two buildings in what used to be the Moorish-era city walls. This spot gives one of the best views of Alfama and the river. Backtrack past the Santa Luzia church, and you reach the Miradouro de Santa Luzia, one of the city's official viewpoints (p48). Across the street are two access routes to the castle. There are several outdoor cafés in the area.

8 Museu Nacional do Azulejo

Beyond Alfama, in the eastern Xabregas district, is the Tile Museum (p34), housed in a stunning former 16th-century convent with an elaborately decorated church.

ST ANTHONY OF THE SARDINES

The celebration of St Anthony on 12 June, falls close to the feast days of other saints (São João and São Pedro, or John and Peter), resulting in a two-week party known as the *Festas dos Santos Populares*. In fact, the city has declared the whole month Festas da Cidade. But the real party is in Largo de São Miguel on 12 June, when grills are loaded, the wine and beer flow freely, and bands play.

Stairway decorated with *azulejo* at the Museu Nacional do Azulejo

Highlights include a small Manueline cloister, a 23-m (75-ft) panel of painted tiles showing Lisbon in the 1740s, and extensive collections of Moorish and Portuguese tiles. The café-restaurant is a pleasant place to take a break.

9 Fundação Ricardo do Espírito Santo Silva

P4 ☐ Largo das Portas do Sol 2 ☐ 10am–5pm Wed–Mon **W** fress.pt ✦

Named after the banker who bequeathed a 17th-century Alfama palace filled with his collections of decorative arts, this museum displays an extensive collection of Portuguese, French and English furniture in period settings. Next door are workshops for traditional crafts such as cabinet-making, gilding and bookbinding. The foundation also runs two schools of arts and crafts in other locations.

10 Museu do Fado

Q4 ☐ Largo do Chafariz do Dentro 1 ☐ 10am–6pm Tue–Sun **W** museudofado.pt ✦

Also called the Casa do Fado e da Guitarra Portuguesa, this museum is dedicated to Lisbon's most famous musical genre and to the mandolin-shaped Portuguese guitar. The museum is surprisingly modern, but its life-size replica of a *fado* venue – complete with singer, musicians, staff and customers – has an old-fashioned feel.

Taking a photo of Alfama's tiled roofs Largo das Portas do Sol

ALFAMA WANDERING

Morning

Alfama is really the sort of place to wander around if you want to explore old Lisbon. Here are a few pointers, to help you on your way.

The street that begins on the right side of the Sé de Lisboa, briefly called **Cruzes da Sé** and then **Rua de São João da Praça**, is a good point of entry. There are also some worthwhile cafés and bars here, including **Crafty Corner** (p70). Keep going and you'll eventually reach **Rua de São Pedro**, which leads down to **Largo do Chafariz de Dentro**, where there's a good choice of restaurants for lunch.

Afternoon

To return to the maze, head back up Rua de São Pedro and do a near 180-degree turn at the top to reach **Igreja de São Miguel.** Follow left turns by right turns and weave your way to **Santo Estevão**. Should thirst overcome you, head down the steps to bar and restaurant **Pateo 13**. A brisk walk up Rua dos Remédios and then along Rua do Paraíso will get you to **Campo de Santa Clara** and, if it's Tuesday or Saturday, the **Feira da Ladra** flea market (p59). If it's not, stroll along to the Miradouro da Graça, the viewpoint near the **Esplanada da Igreja da Graça** (p49), and enjoy views of the castle (p22), downtown Lisbon and the 25 de Abril bridge.

Outdoor dining area at Chapitô a Mesa

Bars and Cafés

1. Chapitô a Mesa
N4 **Costa do Castelo 7**
chapitoamesa.com
This music bar and café with circus-inspired decor has fantastic views over the city and the Tagus.

2. Basílio
N5 **Rua dos Bacalhoeiros**
ilovenicolau.com/en
Enjoy breakfast or a mid-afternoon snack at this café. Basílio offers pancakes, eggs and granola bowls, along with coffee and smoothies.

3. Portas Sol Restaurante
P4 **Largo das Portas do Sol**
This stylish café, bar and restaurant is right by the Portas do Sol viewpoint.

4. Damas
P2 **viralagenda.com**
Set in a former bakery, this inviting establishment is a bar, restaurant and concert hall, all rolled into one.

5. Botequim
P2 **Largo da Graça 79**
A daytime café, which transforms into a music- and poetry-reading venue by night. Enjoy the tapas and cocktails served in an alternative setting.

6. Crafty Corner
P5 **Rua de São João da Praça 93–5** **craftycornerlisboa.com**
This rustic-style bar stands out with its arched ceilings and stone walls.

There are 12 taps, rotated weekly, plus snacks such as chicken wings. Empty kegs have been repurposed as seats surrounding large communal tables.

7. Esplanada da Igreja da Graça
P2 **Largo da Graça**
One of Lisbon's best café-table views is to be had from the esplanade by the vast Graça church (p46). It is particularly attractive in the late afternoon on a sunny day.

8. Vino Vero
H3 **Travessa do Monte 30**
vinovero.wine
This well-stocked Italian wine bar landed in the Graça neighbourhood in 2019. It focuses on natural wines, which pair perfectly with the charcuterie and cheese boards.

9. Outro Lado
N5 **Beco do Arco Escuro 1**
outrolado.beer
Situated right next to Lisbon's cathedral, this refreshing oasis offers different types of beer and has 15 craft beers on tap.

10. Bom Bom Bom
H3 **Rue Angelina Vidal 5**
Mon & Tue
Natural wines and small plates are accompanied by low-key DJ sets at this relaxed bar-restaurant, which has an in-house record store.

Restaurants

1. Taberna Sal Grosso
R3 ◻ Calçada do Forte 22
◻ letsumai.com · €€
Close to the National Pantheon, this
tavern serves delicious fresh fish.

2. Casanova
R3 ◻ Avenida Infante Dom
Henrique/Cais da Pedra, Armazém B,
Loja 7 ◻ pizzeriacasanova.pt · €€
Some of Lisbon's best pizzas are served
at this lively restaurant with a terrace on
the quay. Arrive early to avoid waiting.

3. Zé da Mouraria
G4 ◻ Rua João do Outeiro 24
📞 21 886 5436 ◻ Sun · €€
Famed for its enormous portions of
cod perfectly cooked with chickpeas
and potatoes, Zé da Mouraria serves
hearty Portuguese food at very
fair prices.

4. O Velho Eurico
G4 ◻ Largo São Cristóvão 3
◻ Mon ◻ reservas.ovelhoeurico@
gmail.com · €€
This no-frills restaurant serves a mix
of traditional Portuguese staples. You
can order a few dishes to share, but
the *arroz de pato* (duck rice) is a must-
try. Reservations by email.

5. Arco do Castelo
N4 ◻ Rua do Chão da Feira 25
📞 218 876 598 ◻ Sun · €€
Genuine Goan restaurants like this one
are quite a rarity. Try specialities like

*A fado vadio (amateur fado)
performance at the A Baíuca*

sarapatel (a spicy stew made with
meat, offal, blood and vinegar).

6. Faz Figura
R3 ◻ Rua do Paraíso 15B ◻ Mon &
Sun D ◻ fazfigura.com · €€€
Dig into delicious food here and enjoy
the wonderful panoramic views of the
River Tagus from the large terrace.

7. Lautasco
Q4 ◻ Beco do Azinhal 7A (off
Rua de São Pedro) 📞 218 860 173
◻ Sun · €€
Traditional Portuguese fare is the
speciality of this informal restaurant,
decorated with rustic wooden panels.

8. Santa Clara dos Cogumelos
Q2 ◻ Campo de Santa Clara 7
◻ L Tue–Fri, Sun & Mon ◻ santaclara
doscogumelos.com · €€
Inside the Santa Clara market, this
restaurant specializes in mushroom
dishes (some meaty, some meat-free)
served with views over the river.

9. Do Vigário
H4 ◻ Rua do Vigário 74
📞 916 294 676 ◻ L, Sun & Mon · €
Crates with new and old records sit
alongside the tables at this cosy
restaurant. The menu lists a delicious
selection of Portuguese tapas.

10. A Baíuca
H4 ◻ Rua de São Miguel 20
📞 939 457 098 ◻ L, Tue & Wed · €€
This tiny restaurant serves up a
delicious *bacalhau assado* (roasted salt
cod). The amateur *fado* performances
add to the traditional ambience.

BAIXA TO RESTAURADORES

From the early 16th to mid-18th centuries, Lisbon's royal palace stood on the riverbank, around today's Praça do Comércio. It was the grand entrance to Lisbon, one of the world's great cities. Then in 1755 the earth shook, the ocean rose and fires raged – and the Paço Real and most of the medieval jumble of buildings behind it were gone. The Baixa we see today was built on the ruins of lower Lisbon. Now the heart of the city, it's a lovely place to stroll, shop or have something to eat.

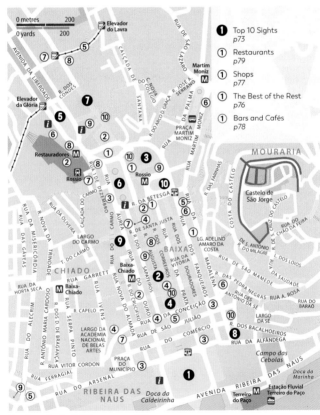

1 Top 10 Sights
p73

1 Restaurants
p79

1 Shops
p77

1 The Best of the Rest
p76

1 Bars and Cafés
p78

For places to stay in this area, see p114

1 Praça do Comércio
⚐ M5

The broad riverfront square, also known as Terreiro do Paço, has regained much of its stature since cars were prohibited from parking there. It is surrounded on three sides by the elegant arcades of Pombal's reconstruction, and faces the river along the fourth. In the square there is a statue of Dom José I, Portugal's ineffectual king at the time of the earthquake, who gazes at the river from his horseback perch, in a bronze by Machado de Castro. In the 15th century, the square was used as a slave port; visitors can learn more about the city's history of slavery on the African Lisbon tour (africanlisbontour.com).

2 Rua Augusta
⚐ M4–5

Lisbon's longest and grandest pedestrianized street runs through the middle of Baixa, from one corner of Rossio to a triumphal archway on Praça do Comércio. The arch, which commemorates the city's recovery after the 1755 earthquake, was added only in 1873. An allegorical figure of Glory stands atop it, crowning with wreaths the figures representing Genius and Bravery. Below, a gallery of national figureheads includes the Marquis of Pombal. The side of the arch facing Rua Augusta features a large clock, much consulted by the shoppers who throng the street.

3 Igreja de São Domingos
⚐ M3 ⚑ Largo de São Domingos
⏰ 7:30am–7pm daily

Dark and cavernous, the São Domingos church is not much visited by tourists, despite its long history. As a result, it is a good place for quiet reflection.

4 Núcleo Arqueológico da Rua dos Correeiros
⚐ M5 ⚑ Rua dos Correeiros 21 ⏰ For guided tours only, chech website ⏰ Sun ⚐ fundacaomillenniumbcp.pt/en/nucleo-arqueologico ⚐

When a Portuguese bank began renovating its head office in the early 1990s, builders uncovered ancient remnants of Roman Lisbon. Guided tours lead visitors deep beneath the city streets through the remains of what appears to have been a factory for making *garum* (fermented fish sauce). A section of mosaic floor uncovered in a separate structure suggests other, or later, uses.

Pedestrianized Rua Augusta lined with boutiques and cafés

MONUMENT TO THE ENSLAVED PEOPLE

More than two hundred years after the abolition of slavery in Portugal, Lisbon plans to unveil a Monument to the Enslaved People near Campo das Cebolas. The city council chose a design by Angolan artist Kiluanji Kia Henda called "Plantation – Prosperity and Nightmare" which depicts sugar cane plantations. Sugar cane was one of the goods traded in Brazil and Madeira during the Portuguese Age of Discovery. The metal plantation with 540 sugar canes in black lacquered aluminium will be a homage to enslaved people.

5 Praça dos Restauradores
🗺 L2

This plaza and its monument were built when the old Passeio Público was turned into Avenida da Liberdade in the 1870s. It commemorates the restoration of the Portuguese monarchy in 1640. The obelisk is engraved with important dates from the restoration campaign, and is flanked by

statues representing the Spirit of Independence and Victory. The surrounding square is dominated by traffic; shops, cafés, kiosks and restaurants cluster in its lower corners.

6 Rossio
🗺 L3–M3 🏛 Praça Dom Pedro IV

Rossio, officially Praça Dom Pedro IV, has been Lisbon's main square probably since Roman times. Surrounded by some of the city's grandest buildings before the earthquake, it was later outshone by the Praça do Comércio, but remains a restaurant-filled social centre in the city.

7 Rua das Portas de Santo Antão
🗺 L2

This long, partly pedestrianized street has food choices galore. The legendary Gambrinus restaurant sits next to the tiny A Ginjinha bar, and between these extremes is a clutch of seafood restaurants with outdoor seating, plus the atmospheric Casa do Alentejo and the cheerful Bonjardim, known for its *piri-piri* chicken (p79).

8 Igreja da Conceição Velha
🗺 N5 🏛 Rua da Alfândega
🕐 10am–1pm & 3–8pm daily (to 6pm Sat)

This was the grand 16th-century Igreja da Misericórdia before the 1755 earthquake, which destroyed everything but the Manueline portal and one interior chapel. When it opened again in 1770, it was taken over by the congregation of another Baixa church that had been irreparably damaged in the quake, the Conceição Velha. The new church was very modest, and most visitors today come to admire the detailed portal. This features a carved image of *Our Lady of Mercy*, her long mantle held by two angels to shelter kneeling historical figures including Dom Manuel and Pope Leo.

A statue representing the Spirit of Victory, Praça dos Restauradores

The impressive Elevador de Santa Justa

9 Elevador de Santa Justa

◘ M4 ◘ Rua de Santa Justa
◘ Summer: 7:30am–11pm; winter: 7:30am–9pm daily ◘

You may be told that this iron lift was designed by Gustave Eiffel (of Paris tower fame), but in fact it is by Raoul Mesnier de Ponsard, his Portuguese pupil. There were once three such lifts in the city. Today the Neo-Gothic lift (check out the exterior walls of the tower) whisks visitors from Baixa to the Carmo ruins (p83). There are photo opportunities and a scenic terrace at the top.

10 Praça da Figueira

◘ M3

After the earthquake in 1755, an open-air market was set up in what is now Praça da Figueira. It became the city's main vegetable market, and was eventually roofed with iron pavilions and cupolas. It joined Rossio as Lisbon's lively centre, and the scene of raucous Santo António celebrations in mid-June. Around holidays such as Christmas, the square hosts the Mercado da Baixa, a food market offering treats ranging from freshly baked bread to cheese.

A STROLL THROUGH BAIXA

Morning

Begin at the riverside gardens to the west of **Praça do Comércio** (p73), where the old palace steps can still be seen. Cross the square and admire the views from the top of **Rua Augusta** (p73). Turning right on Rua da Alfândega, take in the Manueline portal of **Igreja da Conceição Velha** (p74). Then head up Rua da Madalena, and drop into the **Conserveira de Lisboa** (p76) on the side street of Bacalhoeiros for a souvenir of tinned sardines. Turn left at Largo da Madalena and descend two blocks to the narrower Rua dos Douradoures, where you will find plenty of options for lunch.

Afternoon

Work your way through Baixa's grid, up to the main pedestrianized Rua Augusta. Look out for Rua de Santa Justa and a view of the Elevador de Santa Justa. Next stop is the top left corner of **Praça da Figueira** at **Confeitaria Nacional** (p78). Then walk up Rua Dom Antão de Almada, past fragrant shops selling dried goods. On your right is one of Lisbon's oldest churches, **Igreja de São Domingos** (p73). Slightly left and then straight ahead is **Rua das Portas de Santo Antão**. If you've already worked up an appetite, head to **A Ginjinha** bar (p78) for a cherry liqueur.

The Best of the Rest

1. Teatro Nacional Dona Maria II
L3 **Praça Dom Pedro IV**
tndm.pt
The Neo-Classical building housing Portugal's national theatre was built around 1840, at the same time that Rossio was paved with its characteristic black and white cobblestones.

2. Rossio Station
L3 **Between Rossio and Restauradores squares**
Built in 1892, the Manueline former central station now serves Sintra (p40). The statue on the grand façade is of Dom Sebastião, the boy king lost in battle in 1578.

3. Shops in Rua do Arsenal
L5
A dash of an older Lisbon lives on in shops selling dried fish, from *bacalhau* (salt cod) to octopus, dried goods, wine and some fresh produce.

4. Haberdashers in Rua da Conceição
M5 **Between Rua Augusta and Rua da Prata**
Baixa shopkeepers may be buckling under competition from the shopping centres, but at this string of haberdashers' shops you can still buy a single button or length of lace.

5. Elevador do Lavra
L1 **Largo da Anunciada/Calçada do Lavra**
The oldest Lisbon funicular, inaugurated in 1884, connects Restauradores with Campo de Santana, and travels to the Jardim do Torel viewpoint (p49).

6. Centro Comercial Mouraria
N2 **Praça Martim Moniz** **218 880 904** **9am–8pm Mon–Fri, 9am–3pm Sat**
A six-level hotchpotch of small stores, mostly selling international foods, clothes and accessories.

7. Antiga Ervanária d'Anunciada
L2 **Largo da Anunciada 13–15**
antigaervanaria.pt
Claiming to be Portugal's oldest herbalist, this shop sells vitamin super-cures as well as traditional dried herbs for infusions.

8. Monumento ao Calceteiro
L3 **Praça dos Restauradores**
This statue pays homage to the *calceteiros*, the people who assemble the stones that make up Lisbon's famous black-and-white pavements. It features two bronze figures: a *calceteiro* shaping the stone and an assistant who is holding a giant hammer.

9. Arte Rústica
M4 **Rua Augusta 193**
arterustica.pt
This shop is stocked with regional crafts, such as beautiful hand-painted ceramics and fine embroidery.

10. Conserveira de Lisboa
N5 **Rua dos Bacalhoeiros 34**
conserveiradelisboa.pt
Sardines and other tinned fish come in retro packages at this local store, open since the 1930s.

The Neo-Classical façade of Rossio's Teatro Nacional Dona Maria II

Shops

1. Chapelaria Azevedo Rua
M3 Praça Dom Pedro IV 72
azevedorua.pt

The famous hatter at the northeastern corner of Rossio has managed to stay in business for 120 years despite the vagaries of hat-wearing fashion.

2. Manuel Tavares
M3 Rua da Betesga 1
manueltavares.com

Founded in 1860, this deli and wine store between Rossio and Praça da Figueira is the place to visit for cured meats and cheeses, tinned fish and Portuguese olives.

3. Garrafeira Napoleão
N5 Rua dos Fanqueiros 70
napoleao.co.pt

This branch of the wine-shop chain offers a friendly, personalized service. There's a wide choice of table and fortified wines, as well as some spirits.

4. Silva & Feijóo
M4 Rua de São Nicolau 52
916 487 225

Visit this charming little souvenir chain shop to buy traditional handicrafts from Portugal. You can also find culinary treats such as canned fish and wine here.

5. Retrosaria Bijou
M5 Rua da Conceição 91
213 425 049

Trading since 1920, this delightful haberdashery brims with beautiful buttons, ribbons, trimmings, vivid fabrics and other fine wares, including knitting yarn and an assortment of needles and thimbles.

6. Pollux
M4 Rua da Madalena 276
pollux.pt

High-quality, reasonably priced Portuguese home furnishings and cookware are on offer at this

Chapelaria Azevedo Rua,
a made-to-order hat shop

multi-level department store. Take the lift to the rooftop bar-restaurant, which offers sweeping city views.

7. Discoteca Amália
M4 Rua do Ouro 272
213 420 939

Not a disco, but a record shop, which specializes in traditional Portuguese music. It is particularly renowned for its range of *fado* music, and for its merchandise commemorating famous *fado* singer Amália Rodrigues.

8. Sapataria Lisbonense
M4 Rua Augusta 202
lisbonense.com

At this old-school shoe shop styles are good value and sport an inner label to remind you of Lisbon. It specializes in orthopaedic shoes.

9. Hospital de Bonecas
M3 Praça da Figueira 7
213 428 574

Lisbon's downtown dolls' hospital has been fixing up much-loved toys since 1830. Head here for doll fashions and furniture.

10. Casa Pereira Da Conceição
M4 Rua Augusta 102
ovalordotempo.pt

Established in 1933, this delightful shop specializes in tea and coffee blends. It also offers a selection of delicious chocolates and traditional Portuguese sweets.

Confeitaria Nacional, one of Lisbon's historic cafés

Bars and Cafés

1. Confeitaria Nacional
M3 Praça da Figueira 18
confeitarianacional.com
A Lisbon institution for its splendid cakes and pastries. It has a busy take-away service and café tables inside.

2. Penta Café
M4 Rua do Ouro 115 Sun
pentacafe.eatbu.com
This café near Armazéns do Chiado attracts visitors with its supersized toasts, up to a metre long, and cakes.

3. Nicola
L3 Praça Dom Pedro IV 24
Rossio's premier outdoor café is well sited for people-watching. It has a venerable history and a handsome marble Art Deco interior. Downstairs is a restaurant. Coffee is cheaper at the bar and more expensive outside.

4. Dear Breakfast
G5 Calçada de São Francisco 35
dearbreakfast.com
Eggs are served any number of ways at this all-day brunch place, which also has vegan and gluten-free options.

5. The British Bar
L6 Rua Bernardino Costa 52
britishbar.pt
This was once the Taverna Inglesa, a favourite haunt of Brits from local shipping firms. The British Bar opened in 1919. It has a wide selection of beers.

6. VIP Éden
L2 Praça dos Restauradores 24
Art Deco architecture and head-spinning views of downtown Lisbon are the main draws at this bar at the top of the VIP Executive Suites Éden Aparthotel. Just ask at reception and press T for "terrace" in the elevator.

7. Trobadores
G5 Calçada de São Francisco 6A
Sun & Mon
This medieval-style bar serves traditional Portuguese *petiscos* like flamed chorizo. Drinks are served in terracotta cups or giant horns. Make sure to try the *hidromel* (honey mead).

8. Beira Gare
L3 Around the corner at Praça Dom João da Câmara 4
Best known for its *bifanas* (spicy pork sandwiches), this popular place also serves a range of seafood dishes.

9. O'Gilin's
K6 Rua dos Remolares 8
ogilinsirishpub.com
Lisbon's first Irish pub is still the city's best, with live music on some days.

10. A Ginjinha
M3 Largo de São Domingos 8
ginjinhaespinheira.com
Ginjinha is Portuguese cherry liqueur and this tiny bar serves virtually nothing else.

Restaurants

1. Oven Lisboa

G4 ⬚ Rua dos Fanqueiros 232
⬚ Mon ⬚ ovenlisboa.com · €€
Enjoy Indian and Nepalese cuisine in
this upscale downtown restaurant,
featuring a traditional tandoor oven.

2. Gambrinus

L2 ⬚ Rua das Portas de Santo
Antão 23 ⬚ gambrinuslisboa.com
· €€€
This classic Lisbon address is as famous
for its seafood dishes and "rich fish
soup" as it is for its high prices.

3. Martinho da Arcada

M5 ⬚ Praça do Comércio 3
⬚ martinhodaarcada.pt · €€
Once a favourite of literary figures
such as Fernando Pessoa, this is a
great place to try Portuguese food.

4. A Licorista e o Bacalhoeiro

M4 ⬚ Rua dos Sapateiros 222
⬚ 213 431 415 ⬚ Sun · €€
This cosy restaurant is named after the
Portuguese trawlers that fished cod off
the coast of Newfoundland.

5. Terraço Editorial

G4 ⬚ Rua dos Fanqueiros 276
piso 8 ⬚ terracoeditorial.pt · €€€
With an extensive list of Portuguese
wines, this restaurant has a popular
terrace with incredible city views.

6. Prado

G4 ⬚ Travessa Pedras Negras 2
⬚ L Tue & Wed; Sun & Mon ⬚ prado
restaurante.com · €€
Sample a seasonal menu, paired with
organic and natural wines, at this
charming farm-to-table restaurant.

7. Leão d'Ouro

L3 ⬚ Rua 1 de Dezembro 105
⬚ 213 426 195 · €€
This cathedral-like restaurant is indeed
a temple: to seafood. Specialities are
oven-roasted octopus and cod.

8. Solar dos Presuntos

L2 ⬚ Rua das Portas de Santo
Antão 150 ⬚ Sun ⬚ solardos
presuntos.com · €€€
A traditional restaurant known
for its mouthwatering *presunto*
(cured ham) as well as other meat
and seafood dishes. It also has a
good selection of wines. Reservations
are recommended.

9. Bonjardim Rei dos Frangos

L2 ⬚ Travessa de Santo
Antão 14 ⬚ 213 427 424 · €
Grilled chicken with *piri-piri* (chilli) is
one of the fondest food memories many
visitors take away from Portugal. This is
one of the best places to sample it.

10. Casa do Alentejo

L2 ⬚ Rua das Portas de Santo
Antão 58 (upstairs) ⬚ casado
alentejo.pt · €€
This Neo-Moorish former palace is
home to an association for people
from the Alentejo region. The restaurant is open to all and serves
simple Alentejan food in various
memorable rooms.

**Neo-Moorish decor at the
Casa do Alentejo**

CHIADO AND BAIRRO ALTO

An elegant commercial district, Chiado is home to some of the city's oldest shops and cafés. Many of the area's original belle époque buildings were destroyed by a fire in 1988, but cleverly restored by architect Álvaro Siza Vieira around the turn of the century. Higher up is Bairro Alto – a 16th-century maze of narrow streets framed by the wider lanes and longer blocks of later construction. It may be the district of Lisbon with the highest concentration of bars, but it is also a residential area with quiet neighbourhoods of old mansions.

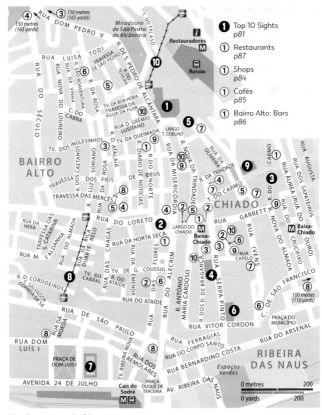

1 Top 10 Sights
p81

1 Restaurants
p87

1 Shops
p84

1 Cafés
p85

1 Bairro Alto: Bars
p86

For places to stay in this area, see p115

Interior of São Roque, the earliest Jesuit church in Lisbon

1 Igreja de São Roque
K3 **Largo Trindade Coelho**
10am–6pm Tue–Sun

The Jesuit church of St Roch, built in the second half of the 16th century on the edge of what would become Bairro Alto, is a monument to the wealth of religious orders and the extravagance of Dom João V – although you wouldn't know it from the outside. Inside, its chapel to St John the Baptist has been described as one of the most expensive ever made. The church's museum of sacred art has an impressive collection of vestments and paintings.

2 Praça Luís de Camões
K4

This square, where Chiado meets Bairro Alto, is a favourite rendezvous point. It is named after the Portuguese poet laureate, whose heroic bronze, with other chroniclers and colleagues in stone around his feet, presides over the bright white stone oval traffic island. It used to be shaded by magnificent umbrella pines, but these have been replaced by still-puny poplars.

3 Rua do Carmo and Rua Garrett
L4

Chiado's main arteries flow at right angles to each other, meeting in front of Armazéns do Chiado, a shopping centre housed in the shell of a burned-out department store. These partly pedestrianized and sometimes steeply inclined streets are among Lisbon's most bustling. Walk up from Baixa to the top, where the café A Brasileira (p85) awaits.

4 Teatro Nacional de São Carlos
L5 **Rua Serpa Pinto 9** **Hours vary, chech website** **tnsc.pt**

Lisbon's opera house, dating from 1793, is regarded as the city's first Neo-Classical building. Its grand façade – the only side of the building decorated, in keeping with post-earthquake regulations – takes its cue from Milan's La Scala, although the floorplan resembles that of Naples' San Carlo opera. The grand interior owes more to the Baroque, with its gilt wood and marble. Outside, on the square the opera house sits on, is a statue dedicated to the writer Fernando Pessoa, who was born in one of the houses that line the square.

5 Calçada do Duque
L3

This series of steps, from Largo Trindade Coelho to the bottom of Calçada do Carmo, is a treat. Along the gradual descent are Café Buenos Aires (p55) and a number of other restaurants. The view of the Castelo de São Jorge above Rossio is perfectly framed.

6 Museu Nacional de Arte Contemporânea do Chiado (MNAC)

📍 L5 🏠 Rua Serpa Pinto 4 🕐 10am–1pm & 2–6pm Tue–Fri, 10am–2pm & 3–6pm Sat & Sun 🌐 museuarte contemporanea.gov.pt 🔗

Located near the Academy of Fine Arts, this is one of the best places to view Portuguese art from the mid-19th century on. The core collection focuses on the 1850–1950 period, but more recent acquisitions and temporary shows bring things up to date.

7 Mercado da Ribeira

📍 K5 🏠 Avenida 24 de Julho 📞 210 607 403 🕐 Food hall: 10am–midnight Thu–Sun (to 1am Fri & Sat); Fish, fruit and vegetable market: 6am–2pm Mon–Sat

Downtown Lisbon's main fish, fruit and vegetable market is a riot of fresh produce. It also has a hugely popular food hall (Time Out Market), home to mini versions of Lisbon's top restaurants, centred around communal seating.

8 Elevador da Bica

📍 K4 🏠 Largo do Calhariz at Rua da Bica Duarte Belo 🕐 7am–9pm Mon–Sat, 9am–9pm Sun & public hols 🔗

Opened in 1892, this is the smallest of Lisbon's funiculars, passing through

LISBON'S BOHEMIAN DISTRICT

Bairro Alto's reputation for pleasure goes back several centuries. Even when this was a smart residential district in the 17th and 18th centuries, it had a notorious side. In the 19th century, after newspaper offices and shops moved in, the authorities made Bairro Alto a zone of regulated prostitution. Today the area is the heart of the city's nightlife, with *fado* houses and bars lining the streets.

the lively neighbourhood of Bica on its way between Largo do Calhariz and Rua de São Paulo. Like Lisbon's other funiculars, it is powered by an electric motor, which moves the cable to which both cars are attached so that they counterbalance each other and lighten the motor's load.

Exploring the intriguing Museu Arqueológico do Carmo

9 Museu Arqueológico do Carmo

◯ L4 ◯ 10am–7pm Mon–Sat (winter: 10am–6pm) 🔗

Accessible from Baixa either by walking or by using the Elevador de Santa Justa (p75), the ruins of the 14th-century Carmo church act as a memorial to the 1755 earthquake, which destroyed much of the structure (p47). The quiet square in front of the church seems an unlikely setting for one of the most dramatic events in modern Portuguese history. It was here that army tanks threatened the barracks of the National Guard on 25 April 1974.

10 Elevador da Glória

◯ K3 ◯ Praça dos Restauradores at Calçada da Glória ◯ 7:15am–11:55pm Mon–Fri, 8:45–11:55pm Sat, 9:15am–11:55pm Sun & public hols 🔗

Lisbon's best-known and now its busiest funicular links Restauradores with Bairro Alto. The second to be built, it was inaugurated in 1885. Formerly, the cars were open-top double-deckers, propelled by cog-rail and cable, with a water counterweight. Later on, steam power was used, but in 1915 the Glória went electric.

The Elevador da Bica tram climbing a steep city street

CHIADO TO BAIRRO ALTO AND BICA

Morning

Begin by the **Carmo** (p83) ruins. If you're coming from Baixa, take the Elevador de Santa Justa or walk up. Crossing to the bottom left-hand corner of the square, take Travessa do Carmo, stopping for coffee at **Caffe di Marzano** (p85) around the corner. Cross Largo Rafael Bordalo Pinheiro to Rua da Trindade and then Rua Nova da Trindade, on which turn right. Passing the **Cervejaria Trindade**, you soon reach the top of **Calçada do Duque**. Straight ahead is **Igreja de São Roque** (p81). Past the church, the street leads to the **Elevador da Glória** and to the **Miradouro de São Pedro de Alcântara** (p48), a garden with great views. For lunch, try **Lost In** at no 56D, or the steak house **La Paparrucha** at no 18/20.

Afternoon

After lunch, stroll along Bairro Alto via **Rua da Rosa** on the other side of Rua Dom Pedro V. Here is the top of the **Elevador da Bica**. Ride it down to Rua de São Paulo and then head left towards Cais do Sodré, taking a drink at **O'Gilin's** or **The British Bar** (p78). Otherwise, walk halfway up the steep hill again and turn left to reach **Miradouro de Santa Catarina** (p48).

Shops

Neo-Classical façade of the stylish
Luvaria Ulisses

1. Luvaria Ulisses
⊕ L4 **⌂** Rua do Carmo 87A
Ⓦ luvariaulisses.com
This small gem of a shop is the only
one in Portugal selling hand-sewn
gloves with a lifetime guarantee.

2. Leitão & Irmão
⊕ L4 **⌂** Largo do Chiado 16
Ⓦ leitao-irmao.com
Jewellery and silverware from a
company that was appointed crown
jewellers in 1875.

3. Embaixada
⊕ J2 **⌂** Praça do Príncipe Real 26
Ⓦ embaixadalx.pt
This trendy shopping centre, with 18
boutique-style establishments, sells
a range of items, such as eco-friendly
cosmetics, handcrafted jewellery
and fine clothing.

4. A Carioca
⊕ L4 **⌂** Rua da Misericórdia 9
Ⓦ vegannata.pt
Coffee beans from Africa, Asia and
South America are roasted on the

premises and sold either freshly ground
or whole at this specialist shop. Tea and
hot chocolate are also available; try the
chocolate sourced from São Tomé.

5. Vista Alegre
⊕ L4 **⌂** Largo do Chiado 20–23
Ⓦ vistaalegre.com
The work of Portugal's premier
porcelain maker is wide-ranging: from
modern to traditional designs, and
from tableware to decorative pieces.

6. A Vida Portuguesa
⊕ L4 **⌂** Rua Anchieta 11
Ⓦ avidaportuguesa.com
This attractive shop in the heart of the
Chiado sells the best of Portuguese
jewellery, ceramics and toys.

7. The Feeting Room
⊕ G4 **⌂** Calçada do Sacramento 26
Ⓦ thefeetingroom.com
Showcasing young and local designers,
this concept store sells clothing, foot-
wear and other accessories.

8. Ás de Espadas
⊕ M5 **⌂** Rua da Conceição 117 **Ⓦ** asde
espadasvintagestore.blogspot.com
This retro-chic store stocks an array
of vintage accessories and attention-
grabbing hats.

9. Armazéns do Chiado
⊕ L4 **⌂** Rua do Carmo 2 **Ⓦ** armazens
dochiado.com
In the restored shell of what was
Lisbon's poshest department store
(destroyed by fire in 1988) is the city's
most central shopping centre. The
larger retailers here include FNAC.

10. Livraria Bertrand
⊕ L4 **⌂** Rua Garrett 73 **Ⓦ** bertrand.pt/
livrarias
The Bertrand chain has branches all
over the city; this one is Lisbon's oldest
bookshop, stocking a wide selection of
English-language titles.

Cafés

1. A Brasileira
🅟 L4 🄰 Rua Garrett 120
🅦 abrasileira.pt

The city's most famous café is an Art Nouveau tunnel of florid stuccowork, mirrors and paintings from its 1920s heyday. The tables outside, where a bronze statue of poet Fernando Pessoa lingers today, are among Lisbon's most coveted.

2. Benard
🅟 L4 🄰 Rua Garrett 104 🅦 benard.pt

"The other café" is, in fact, a tearoom serving cakes and pastries that some consider superior to those of its neighbour. Its outdoor tables serve as a welcome extension to A Brasileira's often crowded terrace.

3. Simpli Coffee Chiado
🅟 F4 🄰 Largo de São Carlos 52
🄲 Sun 🅦 simpli.pt

This tranquil café overlooks the Teatro Nacional de São Carlos (p81). Alfresco tables, freshly baked sweets and speciality coffee are all available.

4. Quiosque Lisboa - Príncipe Real
🅟 F4 🄿 Praça do Príncipe Real 19

This ornate kiosk offers coffees, cocktails and snacks, as well as people-watching opportunities.

5. Leitaria Académica
🅟 L4 🄰 Largo do Carmo 1
🅦 leitaria-academica.eatbu.com

This venerable milk bar is named after Lisbon's first university. Its outdoor tables in peaceful Largo do Carmo are popular. Hearty meals are also served.

6. Landeau
🅟 F4 🄰 Rua das Flores 70 🄲 Sun & Mon
🅦 landeau.pt

Café Landeau is famous for its delicious three-layered chocolate cake. Beyond the blue-and-white *azulejo* façade is a rustic interior with an exposed stone ceiling and wooden tables.

7. Caffé di Marzano
🅟 L4 🄰 Largo Rafael Bordalo Pinheiro 32 🅦 caffedimarzano.com

Italy meets New York at this stylish corner café. The menu offers superb paninis and cheese platters paired with classic cocktails, vermouths and coffee.

8. Café Janis
🅟 K5 🄰 Rua da Moeda 1A

This trendy bistro is situated in the same square as Mercado da Ribeira (p59). Open from breakfast to dinner, it serves a mix of French and Mediterranean dishes. The terrace is ideal for a late-night cocktail.

9. Kaffeehaus
🅟 L5 🄰 Rua Anchieta 3 🅦 haffee haus-lisboa.com

This busy café-bar brings a delightful dash of Vienna to the Portuguese capital. Grab an outside table and relax with a coffee and tasty apple strudel.

10. Café no Chiado
🅟 L5 🄰 Largo do Picadeiro 10
🅦 cafenochiado.com

A popular meeting place for writers, musicians and artists, this colourful café has shelves stacked with books and perodicals. It serves a range of delicious light meals. There is a beautiful outdoor terrace with wonderful views.

The coffee counter at A Brasileira, a local favourite

Bairro Alto: Bars

1. Artis
K4 **Rua Diário de Notícias 95**
Artis is one of Bairro Alto's most lived-in bars. It's a great place to enjoy *petiscos* and the buzz of conversation.

2. By the Wine
K5 **Rua das Flores 41–43**
Empty wine bottles decorate this bar's ceiling, but you can get a full one from the menu which features fortified wines like Moscatel. There are cheese and sausage boards to snack on, too.

3. Portas Largas
K3 **Rua da Atalaia 105**
This is the Bairro Alto in a nutshell. "Wide Doors", as it is called, is a rustic tavern-turned-bar, whose party spills out onto the street. The crowd is young, friendly and laid-back.

4. A Capela
K4 **Rua da Atalaia 45**
The decor of this DJ bar combines sparseness with extravagance.

Relaxing in the burlesque-style Pensão Amor

The deep yet narrow space can get extremely crowded – but always with an interesting mix of people.

5. Majong
K4 **Rua da Atalaia 3**
This is a long-established and a very popular watering hole that offers snacks and a good range of cocktails, including the gin-based *primo basílico*.

6. Loucos e Sonhadores
F4 **Rua da Rosa 261**
This alternative bar offers a more relaxed atmosphere than other Bairro Alto bars. The kitsch decor includes mismatched furniture, books and dismantled mannequins. Drinks are affordable and usually come with a free bowl of popcorn.

7. Toca da Raposa
G4 **Rua da Condessa 45**
Friendly bartenders mix bespoke cocktails in this cave-like bar just off Calçada do Duque. The dim lights and velvet seats feel miles away from Lisbon's traditional streets. Many of the base flavours are infused in-house.

8. Pensão Amor
K5 **Rua do Alecrim 19**
Eclectic music adds to the appeal of this Burlesque-themed bar.

9. QAché Cohiba
K4 **Rua do Norte 121**
Lisbon's liveliest Cuban bar promises a real taste of Havana, with frenzied DJ sessions and deadly cocktails.

10. Friends Bairro Alto
K3 **Travessa da Água da Flor 17**
Set in the bustling district of Bairro Alto, this LGBTQ+ bar serves tapas and cocktails and often hosts pop music parties.

Restaurants

PRICE CATEGORIES

For a three-course meal for one with half a bottle of wine (or equivalent meal), taxes and extra charges.

€ under €20 €€ €20–€40 €€€ over €40

1. BAHR

📍 K4 📍 Praça Luís de Camões 2
🌐 bahr.pt · €€€

Head to the lovely terrace for a pre-dinner drink at this stylish bar-restaurant at Bairro Alto Hotel.

2. Alma

📍 L4 📍 Rua Anchieta 15 🕐 Sun & Mon
🌐 almalisboa.p · €€€

With two Michelin stars, Alma provides one of Lisbon's most sought-after dining experiences. Book well in advance to sample Chef Henrique Sá Pessoa's extraordinary tasting menus.

3. Belcanto

📍 L4 📍 Rua Serpa Pinto 10A 🕐 Sun, Mon 🌐 belcanto.pt · €€€

A long-established Chiado restaurant with two Michelin stars and a traditional ambience. The modern menu is sourced from local, seasonal produce.

4. Antigo 1 de Maio

📍 K4 📍 Rua da Atalaia 8 📞 213 426 840 🕐 Sat L, Sun · €€

This family-run restaurant serves traditional Portuguese fare such as *carne do porco à alentejana* (pork with clams in garlic and olive oil).

5. Tapa Bucho

📍 K3 Rua dos Mouros 19
🌐 tapabucho.eatbu.com · €€

Sample traditional Spanish tapas and Portuguese *petiscos* (small sharing plates) at this modern tavern near the Miradouro de São Pedro de Alcântara.

Contemporary decor at
Michelin-starred Alma

6. Tágide

📍 L5 📍 Largo da Academia Nacional de Belas Artes 18–20 🕐 Sun & Mon
🌐 restaurantetagide.com · €€€

This elegant restaurant serves delicious French-influenced Portuguese cuisine.

7. Rocco

📍 L5 📍 Rua Ivens 14 🌐 rocco.pt · €€€
Book in advance for a seat at this popular spot. It has a formal Italian restaurant and a casual-chic gastrobar.

8. Adega das Mercês

📍 K4 📍 Travessa das Mercês 2
📞 213 424 492 🕐 Sun · €

Classic Bairro Alto restaurant specializing in grilled fish and meat.

9. Bistro 100 Maneiras

📍 K3 📍 Largo da Trindade 9 🕐 Tue–Thu, Fri & Mon L 🌐 100maneiras.com · €€€

Hip Bistro 100 Maneiras is a high-end spot for dishes that effortlessly blend East European and Portuguese flavours.

10. Ofício - Tasco Atípico

📍 L4 📍 Rua Nova da Trindade 11h
🕐 Sat–Mon 🌐 oficiolisboa.pt · €€

A chic, modern spin on the traditional Lisbon tavern, Ofício is a welcoming space for local dishes.

BELÉM AND THE WEST

West Lisbon comprises a series of hills on either side of the Alcântara Valley, now filled with traffic rather than water. The city's former aqueduct spans the valley. Opposite, the residential districts of Campo de Ourique, Estrela and Lapa descend in steep steps south towards the river. The waterfront from the Alcântara docks to Belém is straight and accessible, with the 25 de Abril bridge arching overhead.

1 Jardim Botânico

☑ J1–2 ⚑ Rua da Escola Politécnica 54 ⚑ Garden: 10am–8pm (winter: to 5pm) ☑

Central Lisbon's sloping botanic garden was laid out in the second half of the 19th century, replacing Ajuda as the main showcase for flora, due to its more central location. The buildings at the top of the garden now house various museums, including the child-friendly Natural History and Science Museum (*p55*).

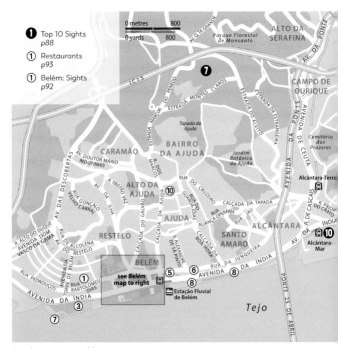

- **1** Top 10 Sights
  p88
- **①** Restaurants
  p93
- **①** Belém: Sights
  p92

For places to stay in this area, see p116

Scenic waterfront suburb of Belém

2 Belém
Lisbon's westernmost district retains pleasant contrasts with the city centre. Refreshing river breezes along the area's promenade and some of Lisbon's main sights (p92) contribute to Belém's appeal, along with its lovely restaurants.

3 Estrela
📍 E4 🏛 Praça da Estrela
The area between Campo de Ourique and Lapa takes its name from the Basílica da Estrela (p46), opposite the entrance to central Lisbon's most agreeable park, Jardim da Estrela. It is a distinctly British part of Lisbon, with the British embassy and English Cemetery (where English writer Henry Fielding is buried) close by.

4 Casa Fernando Pessoa
📍 E4 🏛 Rua Coelho da Rocha 16–18 🕐 10am–6pm Tue–Sun
🌐 casafernandopessoa.pt 🔗

Portugal's great modernist poet Fernando Pessoa lived in this building from 1920 until his death in 1935. Later acquired and comprehensively redesigned by the city council, in 1993 it opened as a museum dedicated to Pessoa and to poetry. It houses the poet's personal library, books about him, and a collection of Portuguese and foreign poetry. There is also a space for temporary exhibitions and events, some of Pessoa's furniture, and the poet's room, which is "recreated" at irregular intervals by invited artists. There's a restaurant in the small, modernist-style back garden.

The art gallery at Casa Fernando Pessoa

5 Assembleia da República
F4 **Rua de São Bento**
213 910 843

This impressive building has been the seat of the Portuguese parliament since 1833, when the Benedictine monks of the Convento de São Bento da Saúde were evicted – a year before the dissolution of religious orders. The vast monastery was adapted in fits and starts; today's formal Neo-Classical building was designed at the end of the 19th century.

6 Museu da Marioneta
F5 **Rua da Esperança 146 (Convento das Bernardas)** **213 942 810** **10am–6pm Tue–Sun**

Lisbon's intriguing Puppet Museum houses a collection of over 400 puppets from all over the world, as well as scenery, props and machinery for puppet shows. It is housed in a former convent, which it shares with the gourmet restaurant A Travessa. The museum also puts on shows and has puppet making workshops for school groups.

A mask in the Museu da Marioneta

7 Monsanto
D2

Leafy and green, Monsanto is Lisbon's largest wooded area and its highest hill. Popular with runners, it is the best place in central Lisbon for the smell of pine trees, a fresh breeze, and a walk with soil underfoot. Fitness equipment has been installed and paths have been laid out for walking and cycling. There are a number of fenced-off recreational areas, including children's parks (*p54*), tennis courts, a shooting range, a campsite and a rugby pitch. It's an area well worth exploring.

A GOLDEN GATE FOR EUROPE

By the time the steel suspension bridge was built across the Tejo in 1962–6, bridges had been proposed at various sites. Similar in design to San Francisco's Golden Gate bridge, Ponte Salazar is just over 1 km (about half a mile) long, which made it Europe's longest bridge in 1966. Its two towers are just under 200 m (650 ft) tall. Renamed Ponte 25 de Abril for the date of the Carnation Revolution in 1974, it has been adapted to increasing traffic by squeezing in extra lanes. The 1998 opening of the Vasco da Gama bridge has relieved the bridge's notorious traffic jams.

8 Aqueduto das Águas Livres
F3 **218 100 215** **10am–5:30pm Tue–Sun**

Lisbon's long-legged aqueduct was commissioned by Dom João V in the early 18th century, and aimed to increase the city's supply of drinking water by drawing in fresh water from springs at the nearby parish of Caneças. Funded by a sales tax on products such as olive oil, meat and wine, construction on the aqueduct started in 1731, and by 1748 it was beginning to bring water into the city. Officially completed in 1799, it carried water across 58 km (36 miles) of ducting. The system was only taken out of service in 1967. The Museu da Água organizes walks across the aqueduct.

The impressive Aqueduto das Águas Livres

The Temptation of St Anthony at the Museu Nacional de Arte Antiga

9 Museu Nacional de Arte Antiga

Portugal's national museum *(p28)* holds some of the country's greatest artistic treasures, as well as foreign masterpieces such as Bosch's *The Temptation of St Anthony* – a painting about the Egyptian St Anthony, founder of Christian monasticism, rather than St Anthony of Padua, Lisbon's most popular patron saint.

10 Museu do Oriente

◻ D5 ◻ Avenida Brasília, Doca de Alcântara (Norte) ◻ 213 585 200 ◻ 10am–6pm Tue–Sun (to 8pm Fri) ◻

Located in an old dockside building, this fascinating museum celebrates Portugal's links with Asia across the ages. Highlights include a magnificent collection of 17th- and 18th-century Chinese and Japanese folding screens, as well as rare pieces of Ming porcelain and Namban art.

A WALK THROUGH WEST LISBON

Morning

Begin by catching the 28 tram to its terminus at **Prazeres** *(p52)*. Visit the cemetery of the same name, then stroll along Rua **Saraiva de Carvalho** past the large Santo Condestável church, with its attractive stained-glass windows. Drop into **Campo de Ourique** market *(p58)* and pick up some fresh fruit, or just whet your appetite for lunch. Then head right along Rua Coelho da Rocha and visit **Casa Fernando Pessoa** *(p89)*. Lunch here, or at the cosy **Tasca da Esquina** in Rua Domingos Sequeira.

Afternoon

After lunch, walk down Rua Coelho da Rocha, turn right into Rua da Estrela, and proceed downhill to **Jardim da Estrela** *(p61)*, where you can absorb the peace of the park. When you're ready, head for the main entrance and you'll see the **Basílica da Estrela** *(p46)* across the square. After a visit, make your way through Lapa via Rua João de Deus, on the left of the basilica. Follow the tram tracks round and then down Rua de São Domingos – veer off to left or right for extended Lapa views. Return to Rua de São Domingos and continue to Rua das Janelas Verdes and the **Museu Nacional de Arte Antiga** (MNAA; *p28*).

Belém: Sights

Grand Padrão dos Descobrimentos on the Belém waterfront

1. Padrão dos Descobrimentos

B6 Avenida de Brasília 10am–7pm daily (Oct–Feb: to 6pm) padraodosdescobrimentos.pt

Created in 1960 on the 500th anniversary of Henry the Navigator's death, this monument takes the form of the prow of a ship.

2. Palácio de Belém

B6 Praça Afonso de Albuquerque Museum: 10am–6pm Tue–Fri, 10am–1pm & 2–6pm Sat & Sun museu.presidencia.pt

This 16th-century palace, altered by Dom João V, is the working residence of Portugal's president. It houses the Museu da Presidência da República.

3. Mosteiro dos Jerónimos

Portugal's greatest national monument (p24) is emblematic of the country's Manueline style. Dom Manuel I built the monastery and abbey in thanks for Portugal's maritime voyages.

4. Pastéis de Belém

B6 Rua de Belém pasteis debelem.pt

The birthplace of the original pastel de nata is a must for every Lisbon visitor.

5. Museu Nacional dos Coches

B6 Avenida da Índia 136 10am–6pm Tue–Sun museu doscoches.gov.pt/pt

This fascinating museum showcases historic coaches, including one made for Pope Clement XI.

6. Museu de Arte Contemporânea - MAC/CBB

A6 Praça do Império, Belém ccb.pt/macccb

This collection of modern art includes works by Picasso and Andy Warhol.

7. Torre de Belém

For many, this defensive tower is the masterpiece of the Manueline style (p32).

8. MAAT (Museum of Art, Architecture and Technology)

This modern art museum (p44) stands out with its striking wavy structure. Exhibits here focus on the connection between art and technology.

9. Jardim Botânico Tropical

B5–6 Largo dos Jerónimos 10am–8pm daily (winter: to 5pm) museus.ulisboa.pt/horarios-e-precos

This garden of tropical trees and plants – the research centre of the Institute for Tropical Sciences – is an oasis in the tourist bustle of Belém.

10. Palácio da Ajuda

B5 Largo da Ajuda 10am–6pm Thu–Tue palacioajuda.gov.pt

The Neo-Classical Ajuda palace along with its alluring interiors were left unfinished in 1807 when the royal family was forced into exile in Brazil.

Restaurants

PRICE CATEGORIES

For a three-course meal for one with half a bottle of wine (or equivalent meal), taxes and extra charges.

€ under €20 €€ €20–€40 €€€ over €40

1. Nunes Real Marisqueira

A6 Rua Bartolomeu Dias 172
 Mon nunesmarisqueira.pt · €€

Located close to Lisbon's top tourist attractions, Nunes is renowned for its fresh seafood.

2. Solar do Embaixador

B6 Rua do Embaixador 210
 213 625 111 Tue · €€

Expect generous portions of traditional Portuguese fare at this jolly restaurant in a Belém backstreet.

3. Vela Latina

A6 Doca do Bom Sucesso
 Sun D velalatina.pt · €€

This place specializes in creative fish and seafood dishes. Try the *filetes de pescada* (hake fillets).

4. Nosolo Itália

B6 Avenida de Brasília 202
 nosoloitalia.com · €€

Fine river views and a wide choice of pastas, pizzas and salads are on offer.

5. Pão Pão Queijo Queijo

A6 Rua de Belém 126
 213 626 369 €

Facing the Mosteiro dos Jerónimos, this affordable spot has been serving stuffed baguettes and pita bread to passersby since 1996.

6. Canalha

C6 Rua da Junqueira 207
 Sun & Mon · €€

Celebrated chef João Rodrigues has created a neighbourhood restaurant with a gourmet edge at this hotspot, which opened in 2023.

7. Este Oeste

A6 Centro Cultural de Belém, Praça do Império gruposushi cafe.pt/esteoeste · €€

An open-plan restaurant with river views, Este Oeste specializes in wood-fired pizza and freshly made sushi.

8. Café In

C6 Avenida de Brasília, Pavilhão Nascente 311 cafein.pt · €€

Grilled fish and seafood dominate the menu at this retro-chic bar and formal restaurant.

9. Arkhe

F5 Boqueirão do Duro 46 Mon, Sat & Sun arkhe.pt · €€

This high-end restaurant holds Michelin Bib Gourmand status for serving top-notch food at accessible prices.

10. Taberna dos Ferreiros

A6 Travessa Ferreiros a Belém 5
 215 873 837 Mon & Sun D €€

This cosy restaurant offers a modern take on traditional Portuguese food. Highlights include codfish and tuna.

Outdoor seating at Nosolo Itália restaurant

AVENIDA AND NORTH LISBON

Avenida da Liberdade extends northwards from Restauradores at a slight incline. It ends at the roundabout named after the Marquis of Pombal, who became Lisbon's de facto head of government after the 1755 earthquake. His statue stands at the centre of a swirl of traffic, flanked by a lion, surveying the city centre he created. If you continue up to the top of Parque Eduardo VII and look to your right, Lisbon's early 20th-century northern extensions stretch out before you. Closer at hand is the esteemed Gulbenkian museum, while further afield are the vistas of Parque das Nações. The park, which was originally the site of Expo 98, is now a fully-fledged Lisbon neighbourhood. With its contemporary architecture and various other family attractions, the area has renewed the eastern waterfront, which was once an industrial wasteland.

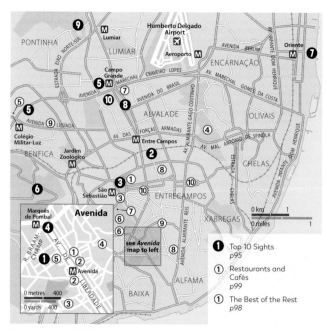

1 Top 10 Sights
p95

1 Restaurants and Cafés
p99

1 The Best of the Rest
p98

For places to stay in this area, see p116

1 Casa-Museu Fundação Medeiros e Almeida

F3 🏠 Rua Rosa Araújo 41
🕐 10am–5pm Mon–Sat
🌐 museumedeirosealmeida.pt

This treasure trove of a museum was the home of businessman and private collector António Medeiros e Almeida, who died in 1986. His collection of some 2,000 objects is astonishing: there are 25 rooms featuring French and Flemish tapestries, English silver, ornate furniture, priceless paintings and Chinese porcelain. Some of the most valuable items include bronze wall fountains from the Palace of Versailles, a silver dinner service that once belonged to Napoleon and a 17th-century clock made for Queen Catherine of Bragança.

2 Campo Pequeno

F1 🌐 campopequeno.com

One of Lisbon's most striking buildings, this red-brick Neo-Moorish bullring from 1892 has onion cupolas and keyhole windows. It stands on a spot where bullfights *(p96)* have been held since the first half of the 18th century. Many concerts and trade shows take place here. Following restoration, a shopping complex was constructed underneath the building; it contains shops, a food court and a cinema with eight screening rooms.

3 Museu Calouste Gulbenkian

Founded on the private collections and fortune of Armenian exile Calouste Gulbenkian, this museum *(p38)* is one of Lisbon's most satisfying sights. Inaugurated in 1969, it was purposely built to display the wealthy oil magnate's bequest to the nation. It contains one of the most impressive collections of fine and decorative art in Europe.

4 Marquês de Pombal Rotunda and Parque Eduardo VII

F2–3

The roundabout where Pombal and his lion pose was the northern limit of the city he conceived. The orderly park behind him was first laid out in the late 19th century as a green extension of Avenida da Liberdade, replacing the pedestrian Passeio Público that the Avenida had usurped. In 1903, Parque da Liberdade was renamed in honour of the visiting English King Edward VII. It is really more of a steeply sloping promenade than a park. For proper greenery, seek out the Estufa Fria and Estufa Quente greenhouses along the park's northwestern edge. A walk to the top is rewarded with good views, the Linha d'Água café and Eleven restaurant *(p99)*.

Expansive view of the city from the *miradouro* of Parque Eduardo VII

Beautiful tiled terrace of Palácio dos Marqueses da Fronteira

5 Football Stadiums

▣ B1 & B2 🏛 Benfica: Avenida Eusébio da Silva Ferreira; Sporting: Rua Professor Fernando da Fonseca 🔗

Lisbon's two main football teams, Benfica and Sporting, both rebuilt their stadiums for the Euro 2004 championships, held in Portugal. Sporting's green-and-yellow Estádio José Alvalade is on the northern city limits. A short distance west is Benfica's red Estádio da Luz. Both teams have interesting museums and offer guided tours of the stadiums.

RIDING AGAINST THE BULL

Portuguese bullfighting is always introduced with the qualification that the bull isn't killed. This attempt to appease opponents of bullfighting is misleading: in fact, the bull is slaughtered after the fight. Bullfighting began before the country's foundation in 1143; however, the first reference to a bull-related activity dates to 1258 and describes D. Sancho I spearing bulls in the north of Portugal. In Lisbon, bullfights were held around Terreiro do Paço, Estrela and Belém. From 1892, all events were moved to the newly built Neo-Moorish Campo Pequeno arena (p95), the capital's only remaining bullfighting venue today.

6 Palácio dos Marqueses da Fronteira

▣ B2 🏛 Largo de São Domingos de Benfica 1 🕐 Hours vary, check website 🌐 fronteira-alorna.pt 🔗🔗

A 17th-century former hunting pavilion, expanded after the 1755 earthquake, this manor house and its gardens are really rewarding sights. The formal gardens are full of statues and tiled panels, from busts of Portuguese kings to allegorical representations of the seasons and the zodiac. Highlights inside the palace include the Battle Room, featuring depictions of battles during the War of Restoration against Spain – in which the first Marquis da Fronteira fought. Fronteira Palace is still owned and lived in by the current Marquis, who collects contemporary art and sometimes stages exhibitions.

7 Parque das Nações

The former Expo 98 site is now a business and leisure area, with a variety of sights (p30).

8 Jardim Mário Soares

▣ C2 🏛 Campo Grande 🕐 24 hours daily 🔗

This popular garden has cafés, a children's playground and sports facilities, which open around 10am everyday. Visitors can rent a boat or enjoy a stroll through this scenic green oasis.

9 Parque Botânico do Monteiro-Mor

📍 B1 🏛 Largo Júlio de Castilho 📞 217 567 620 🕐 10am–1pm & 2–6pm Tue–Sun ♿

Despite its unpromising location, this lovely Italianate park is one of the city's best oases. With its palace – now housing two very interesting museums devoted to Theatre and Costume – it is a reminder of what Lisbon's hinterland was once like.

10 Museu de Lisboa

📍 C1 🏛 Campo Grande 245 🕐 10am–6pm Tue–Sun 🌐 museudelisboa.pt/pt/nucleos ♿

The museum is housed in the 18th-century Palácio Pimenta, at the top of Campo Grande. The palace itself is worth seeing, particularly for the unusual kitchen tiles depicting animal carcasses hung to tenderize. The permanent exhibition traces Lisbon's development from the earliest settlements along the Tejo. Perhaps the most evocative and eye-opening display is the large 3D model of Lisbon as it is believed to have looked before the earthquake in 1755. In addition to the exhibition area, the Lisbon Museum has a temporary exhibition area (Black Pavilion), and a documentation and services centre.

Traditonal Portuguese ceramic in the Museu de Lisboa

TO THE GULBENKIAN AND BEYOND

Morning

Begin at the **Pombal Roundabout**, where you can study its various representations of tidal waves, destruction, and the enlightened despot's many reforms. Cross back to the bottom of **Parque Eduardo VII** (p95) and set out for the summit. If you need a break, dive into the cool of the **Estufa Fria** (p98) and **Quente greenhouses**. At the top, ponder the symbolism of João Cutileiro's **Monument to 25 April** and its contrast with Keil do Amaral's **twin columns**. Then climb the last bit of the hill to **Linha d'Água**; have lunch here, or enjoy a gourmet meal at the adjacent **Eleven** (p99).

Afternoon

After lunch, continue past **El Corte Inglés** (p98) and on to the side entrance of the **Museu Calouste Gulbenkian** (p99), at the north end of Avenida António Augusto de Aguiar. Stroll through the park and exit on Rua Marquês de Sá Bandeira, then take Avenida Miguel Bombarda for a taste of the Avenidas Novas. Turn left onto Avenida da República and walk a few blocks north to admire **Campo Pequeno's** (p95) impressive Neo-Moorish building. Stop for a drink in the park before a spot of window-shopping.

The Best of the Rest

1. Quiosques Liberdade
F3 **Praça da Alegria 48**
Avenida da Liberdade hosts an array of outdoor kiosks, each specializing in a different snack or drink – from cocktails to spritzes, cake to pizza. Occasional live music performances add to the appeal.

2. Avenida Designer Shops
F3 **Avenida da Liberdade**
The former *Passeio Público* (Public Promenade) still hasn't recovered from the introduction of vehicles over a century ago. However, the appearance of international designer shops shows that Lisbon's main avenue has regained some of its pedigree.

3. El Corte Inglés
F2 **Avenida António Augusto de Aguiar**
The Spanish chain has one of its largest complexes in Lisbon. It includes the city's only true department store, plus restaurants, cinemas and luxury apartments.

4. Parque da Bela Vista
Avenida Gago Coutinho
A large urban park, Bela Vista hosts the Rock in Rio festival, which takes place in even-numbered years.

5. Centro Colombo
B2 **Avenida Lusíada** **10am–midnight daily**
Described as the biggest shopping centre in the Iberian peninsula, Colombo has more than 340 shops, plus restaurants and cinemas.

6. Estufa Fria
F2 **Parque Eduardo VII**
One of the most beautiful botanical attractions in Lisbon, the "Cold Greenhouse" has hundreds of plant specimens from all over the world, and sparkling waterfalls and brooks.

Lisbon's sprawling Colombo Shopping Centre

7. Museu Rafael Bordalo Pinheiro
C1 **Campo Grande 382** **215 818 540** **10am–6pm Tue–Sun**
This museum, dedicated to Portugal's best-known caricaturist and ceramic artist, offers a thorough but light-hearted look at Portugal's history.

8. Culturgest
G1 **Rua Arco do Cego** **217 905 155** **11am–6pm Tue–Sun**
Housed in the Post-Modern headquarters of a state-owned bank, Culturgest stages music, dance, theatre and exhibitions.

9. Benfica
B2 **Estrada de Benfica**
This suburb, now a part of the city, has its own rhythm. The football team did not start here – it moved in – but this is still one of Lisbon's proudest *bairros*.

10. Alameda
G1 **Alameda Dom Afonso Henriques, Avenida Almirante Reis**
Alameda's narrow common and its monumental lighted fountain offer a glimpse of Lisbon as it was before 1974.

Restaurants and Cafés

PRICE CATEGORIES

For a three-course meal for one with half a bottle of wine (or equivalent meal), taxes and extra charges.

€ under €20 €€ €20–€40 €€€ over €40

1. Laurentina

⚑ F1 🏠 Avenida Conde de Valbom 71A 🗙 Sun 🌐 restaurantelaurentina.com · €€

The self-proclaimed "King of Cod" offers an exhaustive range of *bacalhau* dishes.

2. Ribadouro

⚑ K1 🏠 Avenida da Liberdade 155 🌐 cervejariaribadouro.pt · €€

This is one of the city's best *cervejarias* (beer halls). Like many, it specializes in seafood, although some dishes are a little pricey.

3. Enoteca LX

⚑ J2 🏠 Rua da Mãe d'Água 🌐 wineex.today/chub/elx/men · €€

The city's most appealing wine bar serves tasty small dishes to go with its wide choice of wines.

4. Psi

⚑ G3 🏠 Alameda Santo António dos Capuchos, Jardim dos Sabores 🗙 Sun 🌐 restaurante-psi.com · €

This vegetarian and vegan restaurant serves dishes from around the world.

5. SushiCafé Avenida

⚑ F3 🏠 Rua Barata Salgueiro 28 📞 211 928 158 🗙 Sun · €€

One of Lisbon's top Japanese restaurants, SushiCafé specializes in molecular cuisine. Black cod is a favourite ingredient.

6. Kabuki Lisboa

⚑ F3 🏠 Galerias Ritz, Rua Castilho 77B 🗙 Sun & Mon 🌐 kabukilisboa.pt · €€€

This Michelin-starred Japanese restaurant at Lisbon's Ritz-Carlton hotel is a refined yet relaxed spot for high-end treats. Fine cuts of Azorean tuna sashimi and a spiced salmon version of *ovos rotos* are artfully crafted in the open kitchen.

7. Eleven

⚑ E2 🏠 Rua Marquês e Fronteira, Jardim Amália Rodrigues 🗙 Sun 🌐 restauranteleven.com · €€€

Lisbon's premier gourmet restaurant, Eleven offers modern Mediterranean food by Joachim Koerper, which has earned it a Michelin star.

8. Cervejaria Ramiro

⚑ N1 🏠 Avenida Almirante Reis 1 🗙 Mon 🌐 cervejariaramiro.com · €€€

Open since 1956, Ramiro is a seafood lover's paradise. Lobster, stuffed crab and giant tiger prawns are among the favourites.

9. Choupana Caffé

⚑ F2 🏠 Avenida da República 25A

Just a few blocks from the Museu Calouste Gulbenkian *(p38)*, this café serves a staple Portuguese breakfast and light snacks.

10. Pastelaria Versailles

⚑ F1 🏠 Avenida República 15A 🌐 grupoversailles.pt · €€

Wonderful if slightly yellowed, this café and patisserie has a grandiose interior, attentive waiters and worldly-wise elderly customers.

The sophisticated setting of Michelin-starred Eleven

THE LISBON COAST

Its Riviera-rivalling heyday may be a distant memory, but the varied coastline from the mouth of the Tejo to mainland Europe's westernmost point has other attractions too. Known locally as the *linha*, the beautiful coastal region has become one of Lisbon's most populous suburban zones – and yet it retains a laid-back holiday atmosphere, making it a hit with sunseekers and surfers alike. Further inland stands Sintra, a fairytale-inspiring town crowned by the gorgeous Palácio da Pena.

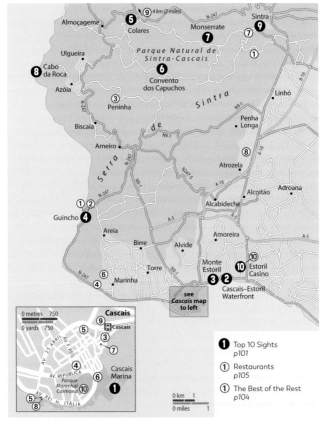

Top 10 Sights
p101

Restaurants
p105

The Best of the Rest
p104

For places to stay in this area, see p117

The marina in the picturesque resort town of Cascais

1 Cascais Marina

Casa de São Bernardo Apr–Sep: 8:30am–8pm daily; Oct–Mar: 9am–6pm daily marinacascais.com

Just beyond the centre of town, and curving around the original fortress on the headland, Cascais Marina has 650 berths and can accommodate yachts up to 36 m (118 ft) long, with a maximum draught of 6 m (20 ft). The many small shops and restaurants also attract a non-sailing crowd. Nearby are the large municipal park of Cascais and the Museu Condes de Castro Guimarães *(p104)*

2 Cascais–Estoril Waterfront

Estoril and Cascais are linked by a long promenade that runs just above the beach, but mostly out of sight of the coast road. By far the best walk in either resort, the promenade is lined with small restaurants and bars and occasionally sprayed by Atlantic breakers.

3 Monte Estoril

The ridge that separates Estoril from Cascais was the site of the earliest resort development, during the first half of the 20th century. It is now a captivating jumble of grand mansions, shopping arcades and apartment hotels – and still manages to be leafy and quiet in parts. Its railway station is reached by way of a tunnel under the busy *Marginal* coast road.

4 Guincho

Still relatively undeveloped, the windswept coastline beyond Cascais, extending to Cabo da Roca, is exhilarating and scenic, particularly at Guincho. The beach of the same name is popular for surfing (although not recommended for beginners), and the broad sands are good for other beach sports and brisk walks. When it's too windy to swim or sunbathe, head for one of several smaller, more protected beaches on either side. Some of the best restaurants in the area lie along the Guincho road *(p105)*.

5 Colares

This peaceful village between Sintra and the sea gave its name to one of Portugal's most famous table wines *(p103)*, now made in only tiny amounts of variable quality. Wine-lovers can visit the cooperative in Colares, at the beginning of the road to Praia das Maçãs, or go out to Adega Viúva Gomes (*adegaviuva gomes.com*), a few miles east from Praia da Adraga. All the same, it's well worth lingering in the older parts of Colares, shaded by plane trees with their peeling, mottled bark. For something different, head to Flores do Cabo (*floresdocabo. pt*), a contemporary art gallery with an organic food restaurant. There are several popular beach spots nearby. Just north of Praia das Maçãs is the village of Azenhas do Mar *(p104)*; to the south is the resort of Praia Grande *(p50)*.

6 Convento dos Capuchos

On road EN247-3 ⏰ 9am–6pm daily (Nov–Apr: to 5:30pm) 🌐 parquesdesintra.pt 🔗

Standing above Cabo da Roca, near Peninha (p104), this 16th-century Franciscan monastery is a striking example of monastic frugality, and thus a rarity among Portugal's opulent religious buildings. The Capuchin monks' cells are small and plain, hewn from rock and lined with cork. The minimal decoration is limited to communal areas such as the chapel, the refectory and the chapterhouse.

7 Monserrate

These lovely gardens, with their blend of natural and artificial elements epitomize some of the essential characteristics of the Sintra region. The artificial "ruin" in the lower garden might have been designed for Walt Disney's *The Jungle Book*, and the rolling lawns are flanked by tropical trees and plants. The Palace (p40), renovated between 1863 and 1865 by English nobleman Sir Francis Cook, represents a wonderful pastiche of Portuguese, Arabian and Indian architectural styles.

Waves crashing against the towering cliffs at Praia da Ursa

8 Cabo da Roca

The westernmost point of mainland Europe is a suitably dramatic clifftop location marked by a lighthouse. Also here is a quotation from Luís de Camões' epic poem *The Lusiads*, carved in stone. The cape is subject to the climatic peculiarities of the whole Sintra region, so take a jumper, even if it's hot when you leave Cascais. Collectors of memorabilia can buy a certificate to prove that they have walked on the continent's western extremity. There is a good café and restaurant, Moinho Dom Quixote, near the Sintra road turn-off, and Praia da Ursa (p51) lies just north.

9 Sintra

To have seen the world and left out Sintra is not truly to have seen – thus goes, more or less, a Portuguese saying. When you visit this stunning hill town, set on the northern slopes of the Serra, it's easy to understand why it was the preferred summer retreat of Portuguese kings (p40).

Stunning arches inside the palace of Monserrate

10 Estoril Casino

📍 Avenida Dr Stanley Ho
🕐 3pm–3am daily 🌐 casino-
estoril.pt

Large and rather loud in style, the
entertainment heart of Estoril is more
than just "Europe's biggest casino",
offering both gaming tables and slot
machines. It has several good restaurants, an art gallery, a varied concert
calendar, a glitzy disco, a theatre stage
and titillating floor shows. The palm-
lined park in front adds a welcome
touch of old-world glamour.

COLARES WINE

Once famous for its velvety,
long-lived red wines made from the
Ramisco grape – one of Europe's few
survivors of the phylloxera plague –
Colares seems now to be relegated to
wine history. Wine is still made, but
very little has any of the qualities
associated with classic Colares. It
seems that the costs of maintaining
the old vines – and of planting new
ones deep in the sand that protected
them from the scourge of the vine
louse – is too high.

A SINTRA DRIVE

Morning

Starting out from **Cascais** (p101),
drive along the Guincho coast
towards Cabo da Roca (road
N247). After Guincho beach, the
road begins to climb. Follow
the main road past the turning to
Malveira da Serra. Turn off to the
left for **Cabo da Roca** or, a tiny
bit further on, to the right for
Peninha (p104) and **Convento
dos Capuchos**. The latter offers
opportunities for walks in the
woods and views across the Serra;
the former an invigorating lungful
of sea air and the possibility of a
drink at **Moinho Dom Quixote**.
Carry on towards **Colares** (p101)
and stop there for lunch, taking
time to explore the village.

Afternoon

From Colares take the smaller
N375 road towards Sintra, which
will lead you to **Monserrate**. Make
an extended stop here, giving
yourself time to enjoy the gardens.
Carry on along the woods to
stately **Palácio de Seteais** (p117),
where tea might be in order.
A little further on you will come
to **Quinta da Regaleira** (p40) –
worth visiting for its gardens and
esoterica – before you enter **Sintra**
proper. Follow the road up, until
you find parking, then walk down
or head straight to **Lawrence's**
(Rua Consiglièri Pedroso 38–40) for
dinner. You can return to Cascais
(and Lisbon) via the faster N9.

Parque da Pena surrounding the Palácio Nacional da Pena

The Best of the Rest

1. Parque da Pena
N247-3 Park: 9am–7pm daily; Palace: 9am–6:30pm daily

The paths in the park around the Palácio da Pena lead to the highest point in the Sintra hills – Cruz Alta, at 530 m (1,740 ft).

2. Golf courses
penhalonga.com; oitavos dunes.com

There are eight golf courses along the Lisbon coast. Penha Longa, between Cascais and Sintra, and Oitavos, in the Quinta da Marinha complex, are the best places to play.

3. Peninha
N247

The Capela de Nossa Senhora de Penha was built at the turn of the 17th century. In 1918 António Carvalho Monteiro, millionaire owner of the Quinta da Regaleira (p40), added a mock-fortified eagle's-nest residence.

4. Casa das Histórias Paula Rego
Avenida da República 300, Cascais 214 826 970 10am–6pm Tue–Sun

Celebrated here are the works of the artist Paula Rego, known for depictions of folk tales and strong female types.

5. Boca do Inferno
Estrada da Boca do Inferno (N247-8)

The rocky coastline beyond Cascais is full of crevices cut by the waves. The "Mouth of Hell" is a deep one, where the waves shoot up a vertical hole.

6. Cidadela de Cascais
Avenida D. Carlos I

The 16th-century ramparts of this fortress enclose several upmarket boutiques and art galleries, as well as a *pousada* which houses the Taberna da Praça restaurant.

7. Palácio Biester
Avenida Almeida Garrett 1A Hours vary, chech website 1 Jan & 25 Dec biester.pt

This 19th-century palace opened to the public for the first time in 2022. The surrounding park offers views of Sintra's top attractions.

8. Autódromo do Estoril
N9, Alcabideche

The Formula 1 Portuguese Grand Prix was held at Estoril's racetrack from 1984 to 1996. Today it hosts MotoGP and A1 Grand Prix events.

9. Azenhas do Mar
N375

This clifftop village spills down towards a rock pool by the Atlantic ocean. It is popular for Sunday lunch outings.

10. Museu Condes de Castro Guimarães
Avenida Rei Humberto II de Itália 214 815 301 10am–6pm Tue & Fri, 10am–1pm & 2–6pm Sat & Sun

This tower and grand villa on a small creek just beyond Cascais marina (p101) are said to have been inspired by a painting.

Restaurants

1. Fortaleza do Guincho
🏠 Estrada do Guincho, Cascais
🕐 Tue–Sat L; Sun & Mon
🌐 fortalezadoguincho.com · €€€
Magnificently sited in a 17th-century
fortress, this Michelin-starred restaurant has modern French à la carte
and tasting menus that feature
Portuguese ingredients.

2. Porto de Santa Maria
🏠 Estrada do Guincho
🌐 portosantamaria.com · €€€
Set in a low, modern building across
the dramatic coastline near Guincho
beach, this is one of the country's top
fish and seafood restaurants.

3. Masala
🏠 Rua Frederico Arouca 288
🌐 restaurantemasala.pt · €€
An informal restaurant, with a good
selection of Indian dishes, including
many vegetarian options.

4. Dom Grelhas, Cascais
🏠 Casa da Guia, Estrada do Guincho
📞 918 500 782 🕐 Tue · €€
Located in a gated huddle of restaurants
and shops, Dom Grelhas specializes in
grilled meat and fish.

5. O Pereira, Cascais
🏠 Travessa da Bela Vista 42,
Cascais 🌐 grupopateo.pt · €
This small, friendly restaurant serves
hearty Portuguese food. The fish
dishes are a highlight of the menu.

PRICE CATEGORIES
For a three-course meal for one with
half a bottle of wine (or equivalent
meal), taxes and extra charges.

€ under €20 €€ €20–€40 €€€ over €40

6. Verbasco, Cascais
🏠 Quinta da Marinha Oitavos Golf
🕐 Mon 🌐 theoitavos.com · €€
Sophisticated modern cuisine is
served here in the airy clubhouse
of the Oitavos golf course.

7. O Pescador
🏠 Rua das Flores 10B, Cascais 🕐 Wed
🌐 restaurantepescador.com · €€
Nautical memorabilia adorns the walls
of this restaurant, which specializes
in fresh seafood. The wine cellar is one
of the best stocked in the region.

8. Mar do Inferno
🏠 Avenida Rei Humberto II de Itália
🕐 Wed 🌐 mardoinferno.pt · €€€
With the Boca do Inferno at its feet,
this restaurant offers splendid coastal
views paired with fresh fish and seafood platters.

9. El Clandestino, Cascais
🏠 Avenida Costa Pinto 10 🕐 Tue in
winter 🌐 letsumai.com/widget/
el-clandestino · €€
El Clandestino offers Peruvian-
influenced light meals and Mezcal
margaritas. Enjoy your meal alfresco
or in the cosy interior.

10. Estoril Mandarim
🏠 Casino do Estoril 🕐 Mon & Tue
🌐 airmenu.com/restmandarim · €€
Part of the Casino complex in Estoril,
this is Portugal's most luxurious and
best Chinese restaurant. Try the Peking
roast duck and the dim sums.

**Diners enjoying the ambience
at El Clandestino, Cascais**

STREETSMART

Pastel de nata and coffee

GETTING AROUND

Whether exploring Lisbon by foot or or making use of public transport, here is everything you need to know to navigate the city and the areas beyond the centre like a pro.

AT A GLANCE

PUBLIC TRANSPORT COSTS

METRO

€1.50

1 hour transfers included

BUS

€2

single journey on bus

TRAM

€3

single journey on tram

SPEED LIMIT

MOTORWAY

120 km/h (75 m/h)

DUAL CARRIAGEWAY

100 km/h (60 m/h)

SECONDARY ROAD

90 km/h (55 m/h)

URBAN AREAS

50 km/h (30 m/h)

Arriving by Air

Humberto Delgado Airport is served by local and international flights and has excellent transport links to the city centre. For journey times and ticket pricing for transport between the airport and the city centre, see the table below.
Humberto Delgado Airport
W ana.pt

Train Travel

Most parts of Portugal are served by rail, with trains operated by **CP** (Comboios de Portugal). Lisbon has four main train stations: Rossio, Cais do Sodré, Santa Apolónia and Oriente. Rossio and Cais do Sodré cover local journeys with lines to Sintra and Cascais respectively. Santa Apolónia and Oriente provide links to international destinations and those across Portugal.
CP
W cp.pt

Public Transport

Carris is Lisbon's main public transport authority and is responsible for buses, trams and elevators. The metro is run separately, also by the state.
Carris
W carris.pt

Tickets

Single-trip paper tickets for buses, funiculars and trams can be bought upon boarding. Electronic passes, such as the **Navegante** smart card, can be topped up whenever necessary or loaded with a 24-hour pass. Cards are sold at ticket offices in metro stations and vending machines, plus some railway stations, shops and newsagents.
Navegante
W navegante.pt

Metro and Bus

Covering most of the city, apart from the west, the modern **Metropolitano de Lisboa** is the fastest and cheapest way of getting around. Metro stations are signposted with a red M, and the service operates from 6:30am to 1am.

Lisbon's bus network is extensive and buses go just about everywhere. They are usually yellow and generally run from 5:30am to 1am in the inner city. A small number of night services continue outside these hours.
Metropolitano de Lisboa
Ⓦ metrolisboa.pt

Long-Distance Bus Travel
Most national and international buses arrive at the main city bus station at Sete Rios. **Rede Expressos** has regular services to most towns and cities throughout Portugal. **Flixbus** also runs regional trips, as well as international connections with Spain and France.
Flixbus
Ⓦ global.flixbus.com
Rede Expressos
Ⓦ rede-expressos.pt

Trams and Funiculars
Trams are a pleasant way of sightseeing but they only operate in limited areas of the city, along the river to Belém and around the hillier parts of Lisbon. Perhaps the most popular route is tram 28, which runs from Alfama to Prazeres in the west via the historic centre.

Three historic funiculars (Glória, Bica and Lavra) carry Lisboetas up several of the city's steepest hills. The Elevador de Santa Justa is an enjoyable tourist experience, but queues can be long.

Ferries
The frequent commuter ferries over the Tagus, which depart roughly every 15 minutes, make for a fun excursion to the port suburb of Cacilhas. Most ferry services are run by **Transtejo**

and depart regularly from Cais do Sodré, Terreiro do Paço and Belém.
Transtejo
Ⓦ ttsl.pt

Taxis
Lisbon's taxis are relatively inexpensive compared to the rest of Europe. Taxis can be hailed in the street and at taxi ranks; most drivers only accept cash. A green light indicates that the taxi is available and two green lights mean a higher rate. Two large firms are **Cooptáxis** and **Retalis Radio Taxis**.
Cooptáxis
Ⓦ cooptaxis.pt
Retalis Radio Taxis
Ⓦ retalis.pt

Driving in Lisbon
Lisbon's central streets are narrow and congested, so driving is not recommended. There are several car parks, as well as metered on-street parking.

Cycling
Lisbon's hilly terrain does not make for easy cycling, but cycle paths do exist. The vast Monsanto Forest Park can provide quieter roads, and there are several popular routes south of the river. A growing number of companies, including **Lisbon Bike Rentals**, now offer electric bikes.
Lisbon Bike Rentals
Ⓦ lisbonbikerentals.com

Walking
Wandering around Lisbon's pretty streets is one of the most enjoyable aspects of the city, and the main sights are generally within walking distance of one another. However, the streets are notoriously steep and can get slippery in the rain.

GETTING TO AND FROM THE AIRPORT			
Airport	**Transport**	**Price**	**Journey Time**
Humberto Delgado Airport	Metro	€1.45	25 mins
	Bus (Aerobus)	€3.60	35 mins
	Taxi	€20	30 mins

PRACTICAL INFORMATION

A little local know-how goes a long way in Lisbon. On these pages you can find all the essential advice and information you will need to make the most of your trip to this city.

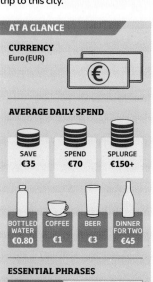

AT A GLANCE

CURRENCY
Euro (EUR)

AVERAGE DAILY SPEND

SAVE	SPEND	SPLURGE
€35	€70	€150+

BOTTLED WATER	COFFEE	BEER	DINNER FOR TWO
€0.80	€1	€3	€45

ESSENTIAL PHRASES

Hello	Olá
Thank you	Obrigado/Obrigada
Please	Por favor
Goodbye	Adeus
Do you speak English?	Fala inglês?
I don't understand...	Não compreendo

ELECTRICITY SUPPLY

Power sockets are type F, fitting a two-prong plug. Standard voltage is 220–240v.

Passports and Visas

For entry requirements, including visas, consult your nearest Portuguese embassy or check the Portuguese **Ministry of Foreign Affairs**. Citizens of the UK, US, Canada, Australia and New Zealand do not need a visa for stays of up to three months, but in future must apply in advance for the European Travel Information and Authorization System (**ETIAS**); roll-out has continually been postponed so check website for details. Visitors from other countries may also require an ETIAS, so check before travelling. EU nationals do not need a visa or an ETIAS.

ETIAS
W travel-europe.europa.eu/etias_en
Ministry of Foreign Affairs
W vistos.mne.gov.pt/pt

Government Advice

Now more than ever, it is important to consult both your and the Portuguese government's advice before travelling. The UK Foreign, Commonwealth and Development Office (**FCDO**), the **US Department of State**, the **Australian Department of Foreign Affairs and Trade** and the **Portuguese Government** offer the latest information on security, health and local regulations.

Australian Department of Foreign Affairs and Trade
W smartraveller.gov.au
UK FCDO
W gov.uk/foreign-travel-advice
Portuguese Government
W eportugal.gov.pt
US Department of State
W travel.state.gov

Customs Information

You can find information on the laws relating to goods and currency taken in or out of Portugal on the **Visit Portugal** website.

Visit Portugal
W visitportugal.com

Insurance

We recommend that you take out a comprehensive insurance policy covering theft, loss of belongings, medical care, cancellations and delays, and read the small print carefully.

UK citizens are eligible for free emergency medical care in Portugal provided they have a valid European Health Insurance Card (EHIC) or UK Global Health Insurance Card (**GHIC**).

GHIC

W services.nhsbsa.nhs.uk/cra/start

Vaccinations

No inoculations are required to visit Portugal.

Money

Most establishments accept major credit, debit and prepaid currency. Contactless payments are gradually becoming more common in Lisbon, but smaller shops and restaurants often only accept Portuguese bank cards, and it's a good idea to carry small change for items like coffee or market goods. ATMs are widely available across the city.

Tipping around 10 per cent is normal when dining out or travelling by taxi; hotel porters and housekeeping will expect €1–2 per bag or day.

Travellers with Specific Requirements

Lisbon's hills and narrow cobbled pavements can prove a challenge for visitors with reduced mobility and those with prams. Facilities in Lisbon have improved, with wheelchairs, adapted toilets, and reserved car parking available at the city's airports and main stations. Ramps and lifts are installed in many public places and some buses (marked with a blue-and-white logo at the front) accommodate wheelchair-users.

Some museums offer free video guides in both Portuguese sign language and the International sign system. Others have braille signs (but these are not as common).

Tour companies, such as **Tourism For All**, offer specialist holiday packages, while **Accessible Portugal** gives comprehensive advice on travelling with limited mobility. **Portugal 4All Senses** organizes tours for those who are visually impaired. Visit Portugal also lists accessible beaches on its website.

Accessible Portugal

W accessibleportugal.com

Portugal 4All Senses

W portugal4allsenses.pt

Tourism For All

W tourism-for-all.com

Language

Portuguese is the official language in Lisbon. English is widely spoken, but the Portuguese are proud of their language and appreciate visitors' efforts to communicate in Portuguese. While written Portuguese is similar to Spanish, the idiosyncratic pronunciation of spoken Portuguese can demand several attempts to correctly enunciate even simple phrases.

Opening Hours

Most museums, monuments and public buildings are open Tuesday to Sunday and some may close at lunchtime; check individual websites for specific times.

On Sundays, churches are closed to tourists during Mass, shops are generally closed, and some public transport runs less frequently. Large shopping centres are an exception, with many outlets staying open all day, every day.

Many museums, public buildings and shops either close early or for the day on public holidays.

Situations can change quickly and unexpectedly. Always check before visiting attractions and hospitality venues for up-to-date opening hours and booking requirements.

Personal Security

Lisbon is generally safe but petty crime does take place. Pickpockets work known tourist areas, busy streets and on popular tram routes, particularly the 28 and 15. Use your common sense, keep valuables in a safe place, and be alert to your surroundings. Lock your car and always store belongings out of sight.

AT A GLANCE

EMERGENCY NUMBERS

GENERAL EMERGENCY
112

AMBULANCE
112

FIRE SERVICE
112

POLICE
112

TIME ZONE
CET/CEST
Central European Summer time (CEST) runs end Mar–end Oct.

TAP WATER
Unless stated otherwise, tap water in Lisbon is safe to drink.

WEBSITES AND APPS

Citymapper
Covers all urban modes of transport, including cycling and walking routes.

Visit Lisboa
The website (visitlisboa.com/en) of the city's official tourism board.

Lisboa MOVE-ME
A useful app for navigating Lisbon's public transport system.

Street Art Cities
An app showing the location of Lisbon's street art.

If you have anything stolen, report the crime within 24 hours to the nearest police station and take ID with you. Get a copy of the crime report to make an insurance claim. There is a police station specifically for tourists – run by the English-speaking PSP Tourism Police – at Praça dos Restauradores, beside the tourist office. Contact your embassy if you have your passport stolen, or in the event of a serious crime or accident.

As a rule, Lisboetas are very accepting of all people, regardless of their race, gender or sexuality. Homosexuality was legalized in 1982 and in 2010, Portugal became the eighth country in the world to recognize same-sex marriage. If you do feel unsafe, the **Safe Space Alliance** pinpoints your nearest place of refuge, or contact **Centro LGBT**, which provides support for the LGBTQ+ community.
Centro LGBT
🅦 ilga-portugal.pt
Safe Space Alliance
🅦 safespacealliance.com

Health

Portugal has a world-class health system. Emergency medical care is free for all EU citizens. If you have an EHIC or GHIC (p111), present this as soon as possible. You may have to pay after treatment and reclaim the money on your insurance later. For visitors coming from outside the EU, payment of hospital and any other medical expenses is the patient's responsibility. It is therefore important to arrange comprehensive medical insurance before travelling.

Seek medicinal supplies and advice for minor ailments from pharmacies (farmácias), identifiable by a green cross. Pharmacists can dispense a range of drugs that would normally be available only on prescription in many other countries. A closed pharmacy will display a card in the window showing the address of the nearest all-night pharmacy.

Smoking, Alcohol and Drugs

Smoking is banned in most enclosed public spaces and is a fineable offence, although some bars still allow it.

Portugal has a high alcohol consumption rate, however it is frowned upon to be openly drunk. It is common for Lisboetas to drink on the street outside the bar of purchase.

All drugs are decriminalized in Portugal, but possession of small quantities is considered a public health issue and results in a warning or small fine.

ID

By law you must carry ID with you at all times. If stopped by the police you may be asked to report to a police station with the original document.

Visiting Places of Worship

Most churches and cathedrals will not permit visitors during Sunday Mass. Generally entrance is free. However, a fee may apply to enter special areas, such as cloisters or crypts.

Portugal retains a strong Catholic identity. When visiting religious buildings dress modestly, with your knees and shoulders covered.

Responsible Travel

When enjoying Lisbon's beaches, try to use reef-safe suncream and ensure that you leave no trace by taking all your rubbish with you. Where possible, support local businesses: purchase souvenirs direct from local artisans. Avoid buying *azulejos* (tiles) from flea markets or second-hand shops, as these may have been stolen. The **Lisbon Sustainable Tourism** website has useful information and tips about supporting the local community.
Lisbon Sustainable Tourism
🅦 lisbonsustainabletourism.com

Mobile Phones and Wi-Fi

Free Wi-Fi is widespread in the city's restaurants, cafés and bars. Most mobile phones have good connections throughout Lisbon. Visitors travelling to Portugal with EU tariffs are able to use their devices abroad without being affected by roaming charges. Users will be charged the same rates for data, calls and texts as at home.

Post

The postal service is run by **CTT** (Correios de Portugal), which offers a wide range of services at prices lower than the European average. *Correios* (post offices) are dotted around the city. Stamps are sold in post offices, newsagents and on the CTT website. Express mail is known as *correio azul*.

The main post office loacted on Praça dos Restauradores is open on weekdays and some sections operate on Saturday morning; most other post offices operate from 9am to 6pm on weekdays only.
CTT
🅦 ctt.pt

Taxes and Refunds

VAT is usually 23 per cent. Under certain conditions, non-EU citizens can claim a rebate. Either claim the rebate before you buy (show your passport to the shop assistant and complete a form) or claim it retrospectively by presenting a customs officer with your receipts as you leave.

Discount Cards

If you plan to pack a lot of sightseeing into a short trip, purchasing an official **Lisboa Card** can be a cost-efficient choice. For €22, adults receive 24 hours of free public transport, which includes the train lines to Cascais and Sintra; free entry to 35 museums and points of interest; and discounts relating to tours, shopping and nightlife. Cards lasting 48 and 72 hours are also available (€37/€46). The cards can be bought online, at the airport and in the tourist offices at Praça do Comércio and Praça dos Restauradores.
Lisboa Card
🅦 lisboacard.org

PLACES TO STAY

From cosy hostels to luxury hotels, Lisbon offers a variety of accommodations. The downtown areas – Baixa and Chiado – provide easy access to several attractions; hilly Alfama gives you a taste of medieval Lisbon; while the coast is ideal for a beach getaway.

Summer is by far the busiest (and priciest) season, but spring and autumn can be just as pleasant. Room rates are usually quoted without the tourist tax, which is €2 a night in Lisbon.

PRICE CATEGORIES

For a standard, double room per night (with breakfast if included), taxes and extra charges.

€ under €100
€€ €100–€250
€€€ over €250

Alfama, Castelo and the East

Santa Clara 1728

Q2 Campo de Santa Clara 128 silentliving.pt · €€€

With only six suites available, this minimalist hotel feels like a private sanctuary. Lisbon's iconic flea market is just outside your doorstep, but the hotel's hidden garden offers a quiet respite from the crowds. At the communal table downstairs, guests are invited to share a meal featuring seasonally harvested ingredients from the owner's farm.

Palacete Chafariz d'el Rey

P5 Travessa do Chafariz de El–Rei 6 chafarizdelrei.com · €€€

Amid Alfama's maze of streets is the Palacete Chafariz d'el Rey. Its pink stone façade makes it easy to spot (especially if you're stepping off the cruise terminal, as it's so close by). There's much more beauty to uncover inside this eclectic building, from stained-glass windows to 18th-century tiles and gorgeous Art Nouveau mouldings. The panoramic river views are another perk.

Hotel Convento do Salvador

P3 Rua do Salvador 2B conventosalvador.pt · €€

What was once a convent for Lisbon's devoted nuns is now a spacious hotel for visitors of all backgrounds, with converted rooms suitable for families and people with reduced mobility. The highlight has to be the tiled portrait installation in the lobby, which was designed by the Pedrita studio – across from the hotel you'll find more pieces by contemporary Portuguese artists.

Tings Lisbon

P1 Rua da Senhora do Monte 37–43B tings lisbon.com · €€

If catching the sunset every night is your goal, then this hotel next to the Miradouro da Senhora do Monte is for you. It's run by a friendly Danish couple who live on-site (along with their cats); you may bump into them in the secret garden or at breakfast as you tuck into homemade bread.

This is Lisbon Hostel

N3 Rua da Costa do Castelo 63 mandarin oriental.com · €

Set in a traditional Lisbon house, this eco-friendly hostel is fit for all seasons. The outdoor terrace is like your own private viewpoint, hosting regular yoga lessons and sunset viewings. Meanwhile, the central heating (a rare find in the city) will keep you warm in the winter.

Baixa to Restauradores

Pousada de Lisboa

M5 Praça do Comércio 31–34 pousadas.pt · €€€

Turning historical buildings into luxury hotels is what this hotel does best. Occupying the former Ministry of

Internal Affairs, the Pousada de Lisboa combines traditional features like arched stone ceilings with modern amenities, including a fitness centre, a heated pool and a steakhouse, all within easy reach of Praça do Comércio, the city's central square.

The Lisboans

⚑ N4 ⌂ Travessa do Almada 9 🌐 thelisboans. com · €€€

When a trio of Portuguese sisters discovered this former canned goods factory in 2012, it was completely rundown. Together, they've transformed the building into a collection of modern self-catered apartments. Be sure to pop by Prado, the family's farm-to-table restaurant a few doors down, or stock up on ingredients at the apartments' adjoining grocery shop.

AlmaLusa Baixa/ Chiado

⚑ L5 ⌂ Praça do Município 21 🌐 almalusahotels.com · €

Families will feel right at home at AlmaLusa, where kids are welcomed with treats such as a box of pastéis de nata and the hotel's teddy bear mascot, Almy. The restaurant has a curated menu for the little ones, connecting rooms provide both space and privacy, and the staff is always on hand with family-friendly recommendations.

Dare Lisbon House

⚑ M4 ⌂ Rua dos Sapateiros 135 🌐 dare lisbon.com · €€

Energy efficiency and the use of sustainable materials are at the heart of Dare Lisbon. This eco-friendly accommodation is ideal for long-term stays, with apartments ranging from one to two bedrooms, some featuring traditional tiles or exposed beams. The best part? You can bring your dog along for the ride.

Home Lisbon Hostel

⚑ M4 ⌂ Rua de São Nicolau 13, 2E 🌐 home lisbonhostel.com · €

Surf lessons, walking tours and pub crawls, this family-run hostel will keep you busy from morning till evening. When you're tired of all the action, you can always hunker down at the living-room-style lounge or tuck into a homemade dinner prepared by Isabel, the owner's mother, who regularly whips up traditional Portuguese dishes for the guests.

Chiado and Bairro Alto

....

The Ivens

⚑ L5 ⌂ Rua Capelo 5 🌐 theivenshotel.com · €€€

If you dislike minimalism, then you'll love this place. With its dark wood ceilings, botanical patterns and antique furniture, the Ivens lobby feels like a vintage

library. The decor gets a maximalist twist at Rocco, the hotel's Italian restaurant, where red velvet seats mix with marble counters and dozens of William Morris-style pillows. The bathroom is a true feast for the eyes, where the rich floral wallpaper provides the perfect backdrop for a selfie.

Bairro Alto Hotel

⚑ K4 ⌂ Praça Luís de Camões 2 🌐 bairroalto hotel.com · €€€

If waking up with freshly baked cakes at your doorstep sounds like a treat, then you may want to check in at Bairro Alto Hotel, which also doubles as a bakery. Its extra-creamy pastéis de nata are especially to die for. And there's more: the hotel is committed to accessibility, providing wheelchairs and reading glasses for guests in need.

Hotel do Chiado

⚑ L4 ⌂ Rua Nova do Almada 114 🌐 hoteldo chiado.pt · €€€

When a tragic fire hit Chiado in 1988, it destroyed many buildings, including this one, which has been carefully restored by renowned Portuguese architect Siza Vieira. Light plays a crucial role in Vieira's work, and this hotel is no exception, with its large floor-to-ceiling windows facing Lisbon's castle and the Tejo River.

The Late Birds

📍 J4 🏠 Travessa André Valente 21-21A 🌐 thelate birdslisbon.com · €€€

Run by Carlos Sanches Ruivo, who actively promotes LGBTQ+ tourism in Portugal, The Late Birds is a hotel especially curated for gay men. More than just a place to stay, the hotel offers personalized experiences to its guests, which include anything from walking tours to gay-friendly bar crawls to beach trips.

Pensão Amor Madam's Lodge

📍 K6 🏠 Rua Nova do Carvalho 38 (Pink Street) 🌐 pensaoamor.com · €€

Set in Cais do Sodré, Lisbon's old red-light district, this former brothel has witnessed its share of secret rendez-vous. Guests are invited to stay in the converted rooms, where messages and objects have been scattered to reveal the stories of the women who worked here. Be sure to hit the adjoining bar for a cocktail or the occasional burlesque show.

Independente Príncipe Real

📍 K3 🏠 Rua de São Pedro de Alcântara 81 🌐 independente.eu · €

Occupying two 19th-century buildings, this hotel offers a mix of rooms and dorms, including bunk beds made of recycled wood. The rooftop (accessible through a tiny vintage elevator) offers similar views to the Miradouro de São Pedro de Alcântara, minus the crowds.

Belém and the West

Pestana Palace

📍 C5 🏠 Rua Jau 54 🌐 pestanacollection.com · €€€

When Madonna moved to Lisbon for a brief period, this was her first home. She is one of the many prestigious guests who have passed through the royal suites of this 19th-century palace. Its luxury facilities include two swimming pools, a spa, a fine dining restaurant (housed in the old ballrooms) and a subtropical garden with panoramic city views.

As Janelas Verdes

📍 E5 🏠 Rua das Janelas Verdes 47 🌐 lisbon heritagehotels.com · €€

What makes this hotel so special? It could be the cosy library overlooking the river or the hidden outdoor patio surrounded by lush wall creepers (your breakfast setting). Or perhaps it's the proximity to the Museu Nacional de Arte Antiga, where you can spend hours admiring Portugal's ancient art collection.

LX Hostel

📍 D5 🏠 Rua Rodrigues de Faria 103 (LX Factory) 🌐 lxhostel.pt · €

If you want to stay close to the action (and we mean really close), LX Hostel is for you. Located inside the creative hub LX Factory, it provides direct access to a series of restaurants, shops and artist studios. Pets are welcome in private rooms, and the rooftop terrace is the perfect place to escape the crowds down below.

Avenida and North Lisbon

Valverde Lisboa Hotel & Garden

📍 K1 🏠 Avenida da Liberdade 164 🌐 valverde hotel.com · €€€

Taking inspiration from London's townhouses, the rooms at Valverde feature vintage-style furniture, framed paintings and draping curtains. After-noon tea is served in the hotel's plant-filled patio overlooking the pool, but if you want a taste of the local cuisine, the on-site restaurant has got you covered with some classic Portuguese dishes.

Avenida Palace

📍 L3 🏠 Rua 1º de Dezembro 123 🌐 hotel avenidapalace.pt · €€€

Founded in the 19th century, this family-run hotel has seen its share of history: politicians, spies and artists have all crossed paths here at one point. The spirit of the belle époque is still alive in the decor and the regular jazz sessions by the lobby. Once you've soaked up the heritage of this hotel, head out-side: a few steps away is the Rossio's train station, offering direct access to the village of Sintra.

The Vintage

🅟 J1 🅐 Rua Rodrigo da Fonseca 2 🅦 thevintage lisbon.com · €€

Pretty much everything you see here was created by local businesses, from the 50s and 60s furniture down to the tea cups at the spa and the pencils in your room. Most suites offer panoramic city views, but if you're not lucky enough to snatch one, you can always head up to the rooftop.

Hotel 1908

🅟 N1 🅐 Largo do Intendente Pina Manique 6 🅦 1908lisboahotel.com · €€

Awarded the Prémio Valmor architecture award in 1908, this Art Nouveau building was turned into a hotel in 2017. The conversion was part of a larger rehabilitation project of Intendente, now one of the city's trendiest districts. The hotel's walls became a canvas for Portuguese urban artists like Bordalo II. Look out for his giant dragonfly at the bar.

Mama Shelter Lisboa

🅟 F3 🅐 Rua do Vale de Pereiro 19 🅦 mama shelter.com/lisboa · €

Mama Shelter has become a popular local hangout with its extravagant maximalist restaurant, leafy rooftop, extensive brunch deals and regular DJ sessions. Don't worry, though, it's still a hotel – and a pet-friendly one at that – with rooms ranging from small to large, plus a separate lounge area.

Sant Jordi Hostels Lisbon

🅟 G3 🅐 Rua do Forno do Tijolo 3 🅦 santjordihostels. com/lisbon · €

Sant Jordi is not your average hostel. Instead of plain white dorms, you'll find yourself surrounded by stained-glass windows, patterned wooden floors and Moorish-style ceilings. The private garden is also filled with original tiled features, while the bar is perfectly set up for a nightcap with fellow guests or your friends (group bookings are available if you're bringing the whole crew).

The Lisbon Coast

Palácio de Seteais

🅟 R1 🅐 Rua Barbosa du Bocage 8, Sintra 🅦 tivoli hotels.com · €€€

What do Agatha Christie, David Bowie and John Malkovich have in common? They all spent an evening at Palácio de Seteais, one of the only palaces in Sintra that doubles as a hotel. The 18th-century building has been kept mostly the same over the years, with frescoes, antique furniture and tapestries dotted around its grounds.

Fortaleza do Guincho

🅐 Estrada do Guincho, Cascais 🅦 fortalez adoguincho.com · €€

Let the sea breeze wake you at this luxury hotel on the coast of Cascais. What was once a fortress to survey war raids is now a peaceful retreat offering privileged ocean views. The on-site restaurant earned a Michelin star in 2001 and still carries it to this day.

Palácio Estoril

🅐 Rua Particular, Estoril 🅦 palacioestorilhotel.com · €€

You may recognize this hotel from the 1969 James Bond film, *On Her Majesty's Secret Service*. Many spy encounters took place at Estoril during WWII, which author Ian Fleming – a (later) guest at the hotel – took inspiration from for his iconic character. Since then, the hotel has upgraded its facilities, which include a spa, three restaurants and a bar, plus access to a nearby golf course.

Eugaria Country House

🅐 Estrada Nova da Rainha 155, Colares 🅦 eugaria countryhouse.com · €€

Nestled amid the Sintra mountains, the Eugaria Country House is ideal for fresh fruits and vegetables sourced from the surrounding organic farm. It's open seasonally from March to November.

INDEX

Page numbers in **bold** refer to main entries.

PHRASE BOOK

In an Emergency

Help!	**Socorro!**	*soo-koh-roo*
Stop!	**Pare!**	*pahr'*
Call a doctor!	**Chame um médico!**	*shahm' ooñ meh-dee-koo*
Call an ambulance!	**Chame uma ambulância!**	*shahm' oo-muh añ-boo-lañ- see-uh*
Call the police!	**Chame a polícia!**	*shahm' uh poo-lee-see-uh*
Call the fire brigade!	**Chame os bombeiros!**	*shahm' oosh bom-bay-roosh*

Communication Essentials

Yes	**Sim**	*seeñ*
No	**Não**	*nowñ*
Please	**Por favor/ Faz favor**	*poor fuh-vor/ fash fuh-vor*
Thank you	**Obrigado/da**	*o-bree-gah-doo/duh*
Excuse me	**Desculpe**	*dish-koolp'*
Hello	**Olá**	*oh-lah*
Goodbye	**Adeus**	*a-deh-oosh*
Yesterday	**Ontem**	*oñ-tayñ*
Today	**Hoje**	*ohj'*
Tomorrow	**Amanhã**	*ah-mañ-yañ*
Here	**Aqui**	*uh-kee*
There	**Ali**	*uh-lee*
What?	**O quê?**	*oo keh*
Which	**Qual?**	*kwahl'*
When?	**Quando?**	*kwañ-doo*
Why?	**Porquê?**	*poor-keh*
Where?	**Onde?**	*oñd'*

Useful Phrases

How are you?	**Como está?**	*koh-moo shtah*
Very well, thank you	**Bem, obrigado/da.**	*bayñ o-bree-gah-doo/duh*
Where is/are …?	**Onde está/estão …?**	*oñd' shtah/ shtowñ*
How far is it to …?	**A que distância fica …?**	*uh kee dish-tañ-see-uh fee-kuh*
Which way to …?	**Como se vai para …?**	*koh-moo seh vy puh-ruh*
Do you speak English?	**Fala inglês?**	*fah-luh eeñ-glesh*
I don't understand	**Não compreendo**	*nowñ kom-pree-eñ-doo*
Could you speak more slowly please?	**Pode falar mais devagar por favor?**	*pohd' fuh-lar mysh d'-va-gar poor fuh-vor*
I'm sorry	**Desculpe**	*dish-koolp'*

Useful Words

big	**grande**	*grañd'*
small	**pequeno**	*pe-keh-noo*
hot	**quente**	*keñt'*
cold	**frio**	*free-oo*
good	**bom**	*boñ*
bad	**mau**	*mah-oo*
open	**aberto**	*a-behr-too*
closed	**fechado**	*fe-shah-doo*
left	**esquerda**	*shkehr-duh*
right	**direita**	*dee-ray-tuh*
straight on	**em frente**	*ayñ freñt'*
near	**perto**	*pehr-too*
far	**longe**	*loñj'*
up	**para cima**	*pur-ruh see-muh*
down	**para baixo**	*pur-ruh buy-shoo*
early	**cedo**	*seh-doo*
late	**tarde**	*tard'*
entrance	**entrada**	*eñ-trah-duh*
exit	**saída**	*sa-ee-duh*
toilets	**casa de banho**	*kah-zuh d' bañ-yoo*
more	**mais**	*mysh*
less	**menos**	*meh-noosh*

Shopping

How much does this cost?	**Quanto custa isto?**	*kwañ-too koosh- tuh eesh-too*
I would like …	**Queria …**	*kree-uh*
I'm just looking	**Estou só a ver obrigado/a**	*shtoh soh uh vehr o-bree-gah-doo/uh*
Do you take credit cards?	**Aceita cartões de crédito?**	*uh-say-tuh kar-toinsh de kreh-dee-too*
What time do you open?	**A que horas abre?**	*uh kee oh-rash ah-bre*
What time do you close?	**A que horas fecha?**	*uh kee oh-rash fay-shuh*
This/that one	**Este/Esse**	*ehst'/ehss'*
expensive	**caro**	*kah-roo*
cheap	**barato**	*buh-rah-too*
size	**tamanho**	*ta-man-yoo*
white	**branco**	*brañ-koo*
black	**preto**	*preh-too*
red	**vermelho**	*ver-mehl-yoo*
yellow	**amarelo**	*uh-muh-reh-loo*
green	**verde**	*vehrd'*
blue	**azul**	*uh-zool'*

Sightseeing

cathedral	**sé**	*seh*
church	**igreja**	*ee-gray-juh*
garden	**jardim**	*jar-deeñ*
museum	**museu**	*moo-zeh-oo*
tourist infor- mation office	**posto de turismo**	*posh-too d' too-reesh-moo*
bus station	**estação de autocarros**	*shta-sowñ d' oh- too-kah-roosh*
railway station	**estação de comboios**	*shta-sowñ d' koñ-boy-oosh*

Staying in a Hotel

Do you have a vacant room?	**Tem um quarto livre?**	*tayñ ooñ kwar- too leevr'*
room with a bath	**um quarto com casa de banho**	*ooñ kwar-too koñ kah-zuh d' bañ-yoo*
shower	**duche**	*doosh*
single room	**quarto individual**	*kwar-too een- dee-vee-doo-ahl'*
double room	**quarto de casal**	*kwar-too d' kuh-zahl'*
twin room	**quarto com duas camas**	*kwar-too koñ doo- ash kah-mash*
I have a reservation	**Tenho um quarto reservado**	*tayñ-yoo ooñ kwar-too- re-ser-vah-doo*

Eating Out

Have you got a table for …?	**Tem uma mesa para …?**	*tayñ oo-muh mah puh-ruh*
I want to reserve a table	**Quero reservar uma mesa**	*keh-roo re-zehr-var o-muh meh-zuh*

The bill, please	**A conta por favor/ faz favor**	*uh kohn-tuh poor fuh-vor/ fash fuh-vor*
I am a vegetarian	**Sou vegetariano/a**	*Soh ve-je-tuh-ree-ah-noo/uh*
the menu	**a lista**	*uh leesh-tuh*
wine list	**a lista de vinhos**	*uh leesh-tuh de veeñ-yoosh*
glass	**um copo**	*ooñ koh-poo*
bottle	**uma garrafa**	*oo-muh guh-rah-fuh*
knife	**uma faca**	*oo-muh fah-kuh*
fork	**um garfo**	*ooñ gar-foo*
spoon	**uma colher**	*oo-muh kool-yair*
plate	**um prato**	*ooñ prah-too*
breakfast	**pequeno-almoço**	*pe-keh-noo-ahl-moh-soo*
lunch	**almoço**	*ahl-moh-soo*
dinner	**jantar**	*jan-tar*
starter	**entrada**	*eñ-trah-duh*
main course	**prato principal**	*prah-too prin-see-pahl'*
dessert	**sobremesa**	*soh-bre-meh-zuh*
rare	**mal passado**	*mahl' puh-sah-doo*
medium	**médio**	*meh-dee-oo*
well done	**bem passado**	*bayñ puh-sah-doo*

Menu Decoder

açorda	*uh-sor-duh*	bread-based stew
açúcar	*uh-soo-kar*	sugar
água mineral	*ah-gwuh mee-ne-rahl'*	mineral water
com gás	*koñ gas*	sparkling
sem gás	*sayñ gas*	still
alho	*al-yoo*	garlic
amêijoas	*uh-may-joo-ash*	clams
arroz	*uh-rohsh*	rice
atum	*uh-tooñ*	tuna
azeitonas	*uh-zay-toh-nash*	olives
bacalhau	*buh-kuh-lyow*	dried, salted cod
batatas	*buh-tah-tash*	potatoes
batatas fritas	*buh-tah-tash free-tash*	French fries
bica	*bee-kuh*	espresso
bife	*beef*	steak
bolo	*boh-loo*	cake
borrego	*boo-reh-goo*	lamb
café	*kuh-feh*	coffee
camarões	*kuh-muh-roysh*	shrimp
caranguejo	*kuh-rañ-gay-joo*	crab
carne	*karn'*	meat
cebola	*se-boh-luh*	onion
cerveja	*sehr-vay-juh*	beer
chouriço	*shoh-ree-soo*	red, spicy sausage
cogumelos	*koo-goo-meh-loosh*	mushrooms
fiambre	*fee-añbr'*	ham
fígado	*fee-guh-doo*	liver
frango	*frañ-goo*	chicken
frito	*free-too*	fried
fruta	*froo-tuh*	fruit
gambas	*gam-bash*	prawns
gelado	*je-lah-doo*	ice cream
gelo	*jeh-loo*	ice
grelhado	*grel-yah-d*	grilled
maçã	*muh-sañ*	apple
manteiga	*mañ-tay-guh*	butter
marisco	*muh-reesh-koosh*	seafood
ostras	*osh-trash*	oysters
ovos	*oh-voosh*	eggs
pão	*powñ*	bread
pastel	*pash-tehl'*	pastry
pato	*pah-too*	duck

peixe	*paysh'*	fish
pimenta	*pee-meñ-tuh*	pepper
polvo	*pohl'-voo*	octopus
porco	*por-coo*	pork
queijo	*kay-joo*	cheese
sal	*sahl'*	salt
salada	*suh-lah-duh*	salad
salsichas	*sahl-see-shash*	sausages
sopa	*soh-puh*	soup
sumo	*soo-moo*	juice
tamboril	*tañ-boo-ril'*	monkfish
tomate	*too-maht'*	tomato
vinho branco	*veeñ-yoo brañ-koo*	white wine
vinho tinto	*veeñ-yoo teeñ-too*	red wine
vitela	*vee-teh-luh*	veal

Numbers

0	**zero**	*zeh-roo*
1	**um**	*ooñ*
2	**dois**	*doysh*
3	**três**	*tresh*
4	**quatro**	*kwa-troo*
5	**cinco**	*seeñ-koo*
6	**seis**	*saysh*
7	**sete**	*set'*
8	**oito**	*oy-too*
9	**nove**	*nov'*
10	**dez**	*desh*
11	**onze**	*oñz'*
12	**doze**	*doz'*
13	**treze**	*trez'*
14	**catorze**	*ka-torz'*
15	**quinze**	*keeñz'*
16	**dezasseis**	*de-zuh-saysh*
17	**dezassete**	*de-zuh-set'*
18	**dezoito**	**de-zoy-too**
19	**dezanove**	*de-zuh-nov'*
20	**vinte**	*veent'*
21	**vinte e um**	*veen-tee-ooñ*
30	**trinta**	*treeñ-tuh*
40	**quarenta**	*kwa-reñ-tuh*
50	**cinquenta**	*seen-kweñ-tuh*
60	**sessenta**	*se-señ-tuh*
70	**setenta**	*se-teñ-tuh*
80	**oitenta**	*oy-teñ-tuh*
90	**noventa**	*noo-veñ-tuh*
100	**cem**	*sayñ*
101	**cento e um**	*señ-too-ee-ooñ*
200	**duzentos**	*doo-zeñ-toosh*
300	**trezentos**	*tre-zeñ-toosh*
400	**quatrocentos**	*kwa-troo-señ-toosh*
500	**quinhentos**	*kee-nyeñ-toosh*
700	**setecentos**	*set'-señ-toosh*
900	**novecentos**	*nov'-señ-toosh*
1,000	**mil**	*meel'*

Time

one minute	**um minuto**	*ooñ mee-noo-too*
one hour	**uma hora**	*oo-muh oh-ruh*
half an hour	**meia-hora**	*may-uh-oh-ruh*
Monday	**segunda-feira**	*se-goon-duh-fay-ruh*
Tuesday	**terça-feira**	*ter-sa-fay-ruh*
Wednesday	**quarta-feira**	*kwar-ta-fay-ruh*
Thursday	**quinta-feira**	*keen-ta-fay-ruh*
Friday	**sexta-feira**	*say-shta-fay-ruh*
Saturday	**sábado**	*sah-ba-doo*
Sunday	**domingo**	*doo-meen-goo*

ACKNOWLEDGMENTS

This edition updated by

Contributors Lucy Bryson, Joana Taborda

Senior Editor Alison McGill

Senior Designers Laura O'Brien, Stuti Tiwari

Project Editors Lucy Sara-Kelly, Aimee White

Project Art Editor Bharti Karakoti

Assistant Editor Abhidha Lakhera

Proofreader Ruth Reisenberger

Indexer Helen Peters

Picture Researcher Manager Taiyaba Khatoon

Senior Picture Researcher Nishwan Rasool

Assistant Picture Research Administrator Manpreet Kaur

Publishing Assistant Simona Velikova

Jacket Designer Laura O'Brien

Jacket Picture Researcher Simona Velikova

Cartography Simonetta Giori

Senior Cartographer James MacDonald

DTP Designer Rohit Rojal, Nityanand Kumar

Pre-production Manager Balwant Singh

Production Manager Pankaj Sharma

Production Controller Kariss Ainsworth

Managing Editors Shikha Kulkarni, Beverly Smart, Hollie Teague

Managing Art Editor Gemma Doyle

Senior Managing Art Editor Priyanka Thakur

Art Director Maxine Pedliham

Publishing Director Georgina Dee

DK would like to thank the following for their contribution to the previous editions: Tomas Tranæus, Matthew Hancock, Linda Whitwam, Peter Wilson, Rough Guides/Natascha Sturny and Tony Souter.

The publisher would like to thank the following for their kind permission to reproduce their photographs:

(Key: a-above; b-below/bottom; c-centre; f-far; l-left; r-right; t-top)

Alamy Stock Photo: Mauricio Abreu 15clb, 41crb, 97bl, Agenzia Sintesi / Fiorani Fabio 13clb, 83tl, 84, Alessandro Avondo 89br, Radu Bercan 54, Stuart Black 102bl, Martyn Boyd 31cra, Michael Brooks 35b, 41bl, 68, Rick Buettner 93, Chronicle 10cla, Classic Image 9tl, 14, Ian Dagnall 24bl, 25t, Ian G Dagnall 45, Isabelle Dupont 69tl, Earth Pixel LLC 15tr, 56–57, 75tl, Endless Travel 17, Eye Ubiquitous / Stephen Rafferty 11t, GM Photo Images 27tl, Renato Granieri 13bl, Avenet Pascal / Hemis.fr 39t , Moirenc Camille / Hemis.fr 16crb, Peter Herbert 31tl, Peter Horree 9cra, 91tl, Image Professionals GmbH / Holger Leue 28t, Imagebroker / Arco / J. Moreno 62t, imageBROKER / J. Moreno 15cb, imageBROKER / Jan Wehnert 27br, Bildagentur-online / Joko 13cla, Bjanka Kadic 59b, M.Sobreira 43, 86, Dov Makabaw 85, mauritius images GmbH / Thomas Haensgen 92, Mikehoward 2 36–37t, Mikehoward 3 37tr, Ilpo Musto 71, North Wind Picture Archives 9br, Roman Pesarenko 90–91b, Pictorial Press Ltd 10tl, picturelibrary 13cl, 16cla, 32bl, 77, 98, Prisma Archivo 9tr, Luca Quadrio 79, Reda & Co Srl 107, robertharding / G&M Therin-Weise 53t, Steve Speller 22br, Stephen Taylor 51, The Picture Art Collection 8, Andrea Varagnolo 74, Ivan Vdovin 25b, 31tr, Michel & Gabrielle Therin-Weise 12crb, Dudley Wood 59t, Z1 Collection 10–11b.

Alma: Nuno Correia 87.

AWL Images: Mauricio Abreu 62–63b.

© Calouste Gulbenkian Foundation, Lisbon: 38bc, 39b.

Chapitô: 70.

Confeiteria Nacional: 78.

'Direção-Geral do Património Cultural/ Arquivo de Documentação Fotográfica (DGPC/ADF): Museo Nacional dos Coches 44, Museu Nacional de Arte Antiga 29bl.

Dreamstime.com: Nuno Almeida 23bc, Arkantostock 47, Michal Balada 102–103t, Artur Bogacki 10bl, Alessandro Cristiano 34, Dudlajzov 37b, 40, 46, 89t, E55evu 73, Elenaphotos 13clb (9), Rob Van Esch 26cla, Greta Gabaglio 82cra, Dan Grytsku 55, Sean Pavone 33, William Perry 67tr, Sam74100 50, 61, Rui G. Santos 96, Giancarlo Liguori Pinto Da Silva 104, Smallredgirl 12br, Dmitry Sytnik 52, Tashka2000 82b, Tomas1111 22–23t, 48–49t, Zts 58b, 63t.

El Clandestino: 105.

Getty Images: Corbis Documentary / Massimo Borchi / Atlantide Phototravel 95, Joao Rico / DeFodi Images 13tl, Moment / Alexander Spatari 6–7, 12cra, 101, Moment Open / joe daniel price 19, The Image Bank / James O'Neil 5, The Image Bank / Sylvain Sonnet 81.

Getty Images / iStock: christobolo 48br, E+ / fotoVoyager 30–31b, Olimpia Tosheva 20bl, Silvia Zecchin 20cl.

Museu da Marioneta: Diogo Ferreira 90clb.

PSML: Emigus 41br.

Shutterstock.com: amnat30 21cra, barmalini 12cr, Janis Eglins 32clb, ESB Professional 65, Lydia Evans 28bl, Sean Hsu 60, jimmonkphotography 76, Katvic 32br, silverfox999 21cla.

Thema Hotels & Resorts: Eleven 99.

Sheet Map Cover Image:
Getty Images / iStock: Armando Oliveira.

Cover Images:
Front and Spine: **Getty Images / iStock:** Armando Oliveira.
Back: **Alamy Stock Photo:** Endless Travel cl; **Dreamstime.com:** Sam74100 tr; **Getty Images / iStock:** christobolo tl.

All other images © Dorling Kindersley Limited
For further information see: www.dkimages.com

Illustrators: Chris Orr & Associates

First edition created by Book Creation Services Ltd, London

A NOTE FROM DK

The rate at which the world is changing is constantly keeping the DK travel team on our toes. While we've worked hard to ensure that this edition of Lisbon is accurate and up-to-date, we know that opening hours alter, standards shift, prices fluctuate, places close and new ones pop up in their stead. So, if you notice we've got something wrong or left something out, we want to hear about it. Please get in touch at travelguides@dk.com

First Edition 2007

Published in Great Britain by
Dorling Kindersley Limited,
DK, One Embassy Gardens, 8 Viaduct
Gardens, London SW11 7BW, UK

The authorised representative in the EEA is
Dorling Kindersley Verlag GmbH. Arnulfstr.
124, 80636 Munich, Germany

Published in the United States by
DK Publishing, 1745 Broadway, 20th Floor,
New York, NY 10019, USA

Copyright © 2007, 2024 Dorling
Kindersley Limited
A Penguin Random House Company

24 25 26 27 10 9 8 7 6 5 4 3 2 1

A CIP catalog record is available
from the British Library.

A catalog record for this book is available
from the Library of Congress.

ISSN: 1479-344X

ISBN: 978-0-2416-7616-5

Printed and bound in China

www.dk.com